ON YER BIKE, NURSE

It is 1960 and two young district nurses, one white, one black, are about to taste city life in London. Sarah is Jamaican and when she and Monika finally find a landlady who doesn't say 'No blacks' they settle into a flat near Camberwell. Cycling with a Gladstone bag and a London A–Z from tenement to opulent flat, from tree-lined suburb to neglected slum, they encounter all forms of the human condition. The dramatic and heart-breaking stories of the people Sarah and Monika encounter are based on Rita Bell's own diaries of the time when she lived this life.

ON YER BIKE, NURSE

ON YER BIKE, NURSE

by

Rita Bell

Magna Large Print Books
Long Preston, North Yorkshire,
BD23 4ND, England.

British Library Cataloguing in Publication Data.

Bell, Rita
    On yer bike, nurse.

    A catalogue record of this book is
    available from the British Library

    ISBN   0-7505-2491-X

First published in Great Britain 2004 by The Book Guild Ltd.

Copyright © Rita Bell 2004

Cover illustration © Edge Interactive Ltd by arrangement with
The Book Guild Ltd.

Published in Large Print 2006 by arrangement with
The Book Guild Ltd.

Magna Large Print is an imprint of Library Magna Books Ltd.

Printed and bound in Great Britain by
T.J. (International) Ltd., Cornwall, PL28 8RW

Chapter One

The shed was a den of antiquity, with a motley display of outmoded sit up and beg bikes. It would have helped if my feet came somewhere near the pedals: not only was I mounting a horse, but my feet were dangling without stirrups. This was *not* going to be the romantic *Les Bicyclettes de Belsize*, pedalling around London.

Apart from a London *A-Z*, it had not occurred to me how I would find my way around Camberwell or Brixton when I started my training to become a Queen's District Nurse.

It was 1960, and I was still strapping a black, cracked leather Gladstone to the rear of my bike. Children under seven were confident of the contents of the nurse's little black bag. To the uninitiated, the Gladstone bag has an insert of white linen compartments to accommodate forceps, scissors, bandages and antiseptic lotion. In a separate linen bag was the 'patient's friend' – the enema apparatus with its coiling rubber tubes, glass funnel, glass connections and emerald green solution. What a versatile piece of equipment this could be. Today it could prove very useful for siphoning petrol in a fuel crisis.

When the lavatory cistern sprang a leak, the plumber gazed in amazement at the convoluted rubber tubing trailing all over the ceiling and down the walls. The funnel strapped up with Elastoplast over the leak to stem the flow, with the water culminating in a battered yellow enamel bedpan.

'Bloody 'ell! – I've seen some emergency measures in my day, but I ain't seen nuffink like this. All them bloody brown tubes, looks more like a map of the Bakerloo Line.'

The other bag had a flap over the top secured with a chrome rod and looked as though it was on a journey to the London Philharmonic; the only overture in the music case was the patients' documents. This bag was precariously suspended from a handle-bar and required more than an unswerving resolve to maintain my balance, especially in city traffic.

London Transport buses dominated, with bikes relegated to the gutter. Like an inebriated reveller, before the arrival of *'Blow in the bag, sir'*, I was obliged to proceed in a straight line. Broken beer bottles, the dread of a puncture and the constant fear of wrapping myself around a red double-decker made cycling 'on the district' a nightmare.

Having qualified as a nurse in London, I was restless to free myself from the perpetual petty restrictions of hospital life: the constant checking of bed wheels to make sure they all faced Mecca and Matron's twelve inch rule for the turn back of the sheet.

As Queen's Nurses we were distinguished from other district nurses. Not for us a little nursing badge. We wore an enormous bronze badge the size of a rugby ball – OK, a golf ball – on a long length of blue cord. This delighted most of the male patients, who were mesmerised watching it bob up and down on the nurse's boobs at the slightest movement.

As soon as the nurse bent over the patient, the pendulum would swing into action. It worked better than hypnosis, and had the effect of inducing a trance-like state. Just as the patient was admiring the view, the Queen's gong had a knack of clobbering the unsuspecting victim in the eye.

The badge carried Queen Victoria's crown and her insignia VRI. This was repeated on the cap badge and coat buttons. People could be forgiven if they thought that we were a military contingent, and an elderly gentleman once mistook me for an army nurse. I felt quite proud to explain the history to him and his wife.

'Cor blimey Bert, she don't look old enough to be nursing in Queen Victoria's time, do she?' said his wife.

The Queen's were renowned for special

skills, one of which was origami, in a few seconds I could transform an ordinary sheet of newspaper into a receptacle that could take discarded dressings. This work of art will doubtless have been superseded by the ubiquitous plastic Tesco bag.

Another enviable skill of a Queen's Nurse was her anti-bug manoeuvre. This would be achieved by placing a newspaper on a wooden chair with one's coat folded in such a way that the lining of the coat and the sleeves were unexposed, in an endeavour to refuse entry to any flea hell-bent on trying to find a warm mode of transport to accompany the nurse on her rounds. I can't vouch that it worked, I seemed to be always scratching regardless. The patient only had to say, 'I've remembered to put some flea powder down today, nurse.' That was the signal, I would be clawing at my body like a chimp.

It is amazing the power of auto-suggestion. When I was a student, the tutor only had to mention that she was about to show an enlarged illustration on the board of a *Pediculus capitus* (head louse) to precipitate a surreptitious scratching all round. The louse with its hairy, wheat-like legs when enlarged a billion times, looked more like a long-haired mammoth than a bug. Even the tutor was seen having the odd scratch. It is as mentally infectious as someone yawning, as you may discover when you are reading this.

To become infested 'on the district' would invoke the magnanimous offer of a visit to the local cleansing station. Somehow the thought of a seething mass of sweaty, smelly bodies soaking in a carbolic wash tub was too unsavoury for consideration. Another that occurred to me, there was always the chance of it being the annual gathering of the Camberwell Vagrants, sniffed out by the 'woman from the welfare'. All this was sufficient impetus to send me flea-ing home to a more dignified and discreet delousing programme.

Joe's visit was at the request of his GP Dr Hazel Welsh. On her previous visit, he had viciously attacked her, so she had kept away for several weeks. His condition had now weakened, so the doctor felt it was safe for the district nurse to go in.

I made my way down the steep crumbling steps to the basement flat. The door was casting its final school-green flakes of paint. Greasy chip papers swirled aimlessly in the stairwell. As I opened the door a foetid stench filled my nostrils and sent me reeling, forcing me to gulp in fresh air. The smell of decaying vegetation and human excreta permeated the atmosphere.

The man lay motionless. His bed was a hessian sack filled with newspapers. Halos of bluebottles tormented the silence as they played a muffled hum; their iridescent bodies glinted in the threads of light from the windows, carved by rivulets of rain on grime.

For three weeks he had lain in his own excrement, his body rotting. He had, however, exercised an element of discipline over his other bodily function. Like a regiment of soldiers they were lined up. Beer bottles – dozens of them, overflowing with an unmistakable amber liquid.

To attend to his personal care would involve an assault course. Access to running water was difficult, the tap being buried under a mountain of dirty crockery that had stagnated for weeks. I would have to wade through plates, pots, pans, boxes and tins, full of decomposing food, to find water. Hot water was to prove more difficult and hazardous.

The electric meter needed feeding. It was late afternoon with only a brief glimpse of daylight. Thoughts of being plunged into darkness in these grim surroundings were too horrible to contemplate. I searched frantically in my coat pocket for two shilling-pieces. Life experience had not prepared me for what was about to happen. Slowly I opened the cellar door to the sound of frantic gnawing. Rats... Some scurried, others lumbered and dragged their stringy tails over my feet. A choked scream together with my lunch rose from the pit of my stomach. Spiders' webs like candyfloss netted my hair and dangled their prey.

Later I was to learn that Joe too had spat on society and defiled it with impunity. I slammed the door and tried again – this time one hand held the door; the other the money poised in position for the metal box. I quickly shut the door before the coin could clink in the silver pool.

With the electric light restored, the gruesome sight magnified. I could see that the kitchen floor had flooded, and floating in a few inches of water were more furry bodies. Small bony bundles of fur. Kittens – five of them, dead or dying. All would need to be humanely dealt with by an RSPCA inspector.

Joe was dying too and I had a struggle to find food for him. Fortunately the Superintendent had received a number of boxes of groceries from a local harvest festival. Several boxes had been donated for the nurses to distribute to the poor in the community. Nurses would present a particular needy family to qualify for one of the boxes. I must have pleaded my case better than Perry Mason. The Superintendent, Miss Wright, felt that Joe was such a deserving individual, and I was told to help myself to as many boxes as I needed. As I left her office, she called out to me, 'In the circumstances, nurse. I think you had better take the lot.'

This helped for a short while, then to my astonishment Joe told me that his daughter Ruth lived in the flat above. They hadn't spoken to each other for years. He would not give a reason.

One Sunday lunch-time I decided to visit her. A welcome warm aroma of roast beef and Yorkshire pudding, a typical Sunday roast dinner, greeted me. But the greeting from the daughter was neither warm nor welcoming. A slim attractive person in her early thirties opened the door. Through the opening a rich blue carpet could be seen, fitted wall to wall, with matching velvet curtains. An older pasty-faced man in white overalls sat on an oak Ercol-type Windsor chair, reading the *News of the World*.

Having just emerged a step from hell, I was stunned with the contrasting opulence in the flat above. Before I had a chance to speak, Ruth was on the defensive.

'I know why you are here, you think I am hard for not looking after my father.' She twisted a skein of auburn hair nervously around her forefinger. 'I don't care what you think, I want nothing more to do with him.'

I turned my coat collar up. It was beginning to rain heavily.

'I can understand how you feel,' I began.

'You can, can you? Have you ever lived with a violent, alcoholic father?' She spat the words out with contempt.

'No, but–' I started.

'Oh yes, what do you know? Sod all. You people don't live in the real world. You lot, with yer fancy talk. You'd think you were at Streatham Ice Rink, the way you skate around people's lives, prying and preaching.'

With a sudden flick of the hand Ruth tossed back her hair. She stood hand on hip and in a high-pitched, mocking voice said, *'"I understand how you feel."'*

After a few seconds I asked, 'Surely there was some affection between you and your father at one time?'

She looked at me with an expression of incredulity.

'Huh!' she scoffed. 'The only physical contact I had with my father was on the end of his fists. You're all the same, all talk, telling me how I should live my life and how I should be playing happy families. My father would come home pissed out of his skull and then lay into me and Mum.'

I hesitated, then said quietly, 'Your father is dying, Ruth.'

'You haven't heard a word I've said, have you?' she said, her voice rising in a crescendo. 'Don't you understand? I don't care any more, I have no feelings left for him.'

As I left, she shut the door with a resounding thud. I turned to see two bottles of milk on her doorstep. Cramming one in each coat pocket, I retraced my steps to the basement.

Joe eventually went into a London hospice. In the meantime the dirty squad from the Public Health Department fumigated and did a blitz cleaning up the flat.

Joe did not return. Despite his violent life, he ended his last few days, in peace and comfort, tenderly cared for by the nuns.

Whenever I stepped into a hovel, with bedbugs, lice and rodents, there was always the thought: *it doesn't get any worse than this.* A few weeks later, another would surface to etch itself on my memory.

Many of the dwellings in the area were scheduled to be condemned for slum clearance.

There was a certain irony in the names of some of the properties or streets. Often the grander the name, the more dilapidated the building. Christabella Mansions or Byron Lodge may sound posh, the reality was quite different. Peabody Buildings, too, I imagine its design was attractive when first built. It was financed and named after an American philanthropist who had been influenced by Charles Dickens' description of London slums. Now a dreary, depressing tenement block, it looked like a Victorian hospital with its balconies. I walked along one of the them, looking for Mrs Leeson's flat. No recuperating patients here, resting on balcony beds, instead they were bedecked with washing lines and protruding poles laden with dripping sheets and clothes.

I peered over the iron railing, through a gap in some sodden sheets, to see young boys who should have been sitting behind a school desk, lazing on the iron fire escapes, dropping stones through the slots and watching people dodge them with wry amusement.

Girls no more than six or seven years were playing at dollies, except that they weren't dolls, these were real babies. Dressing and undressing them, changing their nappies, then sitting in the stone courtyard to feed them with grubby bottles that had been rolling among the rubbish that littered the area.

Passing row after row of paint-peeled doors, I sensed a feeling of isolation and despondency. Mrs Leeson's newly painted canary-coloured door gleamed like a beacon and offered a safe harbour in the midst of a sea of turbulence. As I opened the door a matching coloured bird chorused in a corner cage, prompting the echoing in my head of the song *'Yellow bird up high in banana tree...'* Once I was inside the flat the screams of the children and the trundle of traffic were scarcely audible.

'Don't you get fed up, Mrs Leeson, cut off on the top floor like this?'

'Oh no, love, I have my nurses and such a lovely view over Camberwell Green.'

We called in several times a day to instil her eye drops. As for Camberwell Green, it was a slither of grass with a bench or two that afforded a tramp the occasional undisturbed kip. Mrs Leeson seemed oblivious to her surroundings.

Edwin Moffatt was oblivious too. His property was a disused shop in Regal Row. The lettering on the sign over the boarded-up shop was barely visible, but described him as 'Antique Dealer'. The faded wording was an indication of how long his business had been defunct. Del Boy's pad in Peckham or even Steptoe's yard would be palatial in comparison to Moffat's Emporium.

Attached to a grimy grey vest he wore a blue bow tie. A thin grey cardigan with equally thin arms protruding through its peppered holes was looped with grey woollen threads. Hanging loosely from a bony wrist was an Omega watch with a wide gold bracelet, a reminder of former prosperity.

'Would nurse care to partake of some tea with me?' he asked politely, bringing in two chipped, unwashed Crown Derby cups and saucers on a tarnished silver salver. I hadn't the heart to refuse. If I had tipped it on the floor it would hardly have been noticed. In fact I could have wheeled in a motor-bike and side car and that would have probably gone unnoticed too.

Edwin saw his house as it was when he moved in with his young bride at the turn of the century, with its lace curtains, antique furniture and objets d'art. Not as it really was, filthy, with dirty rags draped about, cones of mildewed clothes and stacks of old browned, mice-nibbled newspapers.

It had that dank, musty smell of maggots and mice droppings. I once saw some mice scampering out of his kitchen, doing a limbo dance under the door of his outside lavatory.

'You must be mistaken; they can't possibly be *my* mice. You know me, nurse, my place is always clean. They must belong to my next door neighbour,' he said indignantly.

As soon as Mr Moffatt left the kitchen I would throw the tea quickly down the yellow ochre butler sink. This play-acting continued for some time, with him asking – me accepting.

One morning the tatty gingham curtain which half circled the sink and was as grubby as a boy's handkerchief had been left open. For the first time, I saw his drainage system – one large galvanised pail. There glistening in the bottom of the bucket was my discarded cup of tea.

The curtain had come down on our one act-play.

When John Major, a former Conservative Prime Minister, once referred to his lowly start in life in South East London, he mentioned he had lived as a teenager in Coldharbour Lane. He could have been on my patch at that time. It is misleading to call it a lane: it was a wide, busy, road stretching from Denmark Hill, Camberwell, to Brixton. Apart from the occasional block of flats, the majority of the properties in this road were large Victorian houses, divided and sub-divided (some with only a curtain) into flats and rooms for rent. Poverty and over-crowding were sad soul mates. During the war, growing up in Kent, I often heard tell of the war-time spirit and friendliness of Londoners, helping each other in adversity. With bomb damage and re-housing, what had once been a tight-knit communities had become dispersed. Nevertheless it came as a shock in areas such as Coldharbour Lane to knock at door after door to find such indifference.

The owner was usually absent. The tenants might not know the owner of the flats and there could be a dozen families living in the same house and they would not necessarily know each other's name or even speak to each other.

In a typical property in Coldharbour Lane that John Major could have lived in was a cheerful young couple in their early twenties starting married life in one miserable room. On the landing, at the top of the stairs, was an old cooker. Overhead, looking sadly out of place, was a gleaming modern set of stainless steel cooking utensils, a wedding present from the firm. The boss had visualised them as a useful accessory in a modern kitchen! The couple had to share a lavatory with five other tenants.

It was in this same lane that I had my first accident with the bike, when I crashed into a stationary car. The driver had abruptly stopped without signalling. I found myself leapfrogging over the top of the handlebars and felt my neck slither down the length of the rear window before landing in the middle of the busy road. Lorries and cars were skidding and swerving to avoid me.

The driver was unconcerned and only interested in the condition of the car. He got out, examined his car, got back in and drove off, leaving me shaking, dazed and crying with shock. I felt conspicuous in my blue uniform.

A small crowd gathered. No one made a move to offer assistance. As I lay there, I could hear women's voices.

'Oh look, Mabel, there's someone over there, she's had an accident. Do you think we ought to–?'

'Get an ambulance? No, it's OK, Dot,

she's a nurse we can't 'elp 'er. She'll know all that first aid stuff. She'll sort 'erself out. Come on, don't 'ang about, I thought you wanted to go to the markit?'

Mr Bowman looked out of a top floor window of the block of flats opposite as he waited for the district nurse to call. On seeing the accident he hastily made his way down the stairs to help. Although in his early seventies, his recent marriage to a woman half his age, coupled with regular doses of ginseng, had given him the agility of a much younger man. He helped me out of the road and up the stone steps to his spotless flat. He could see that I was shocked and shaken and suggested a cup of tea.

'Why not take your shoes off, nurse, and have a rest on my bed?'

By now he was gasping for breath, having tackled several flights of stairs.

With a head that felt in the grip of a sumo wrestler, I found the offer too tempting to decline.

'Just you relax on my bed, love. I'll get you a nice cuppa. My wife will be back in a minute,' he added.

There was something about his last remark that attempted to pierce my inert mind. Weariness silenced it. Despite feeling drowsy, I could distinctly hear a key slowly turning in the lock. In an instant I could visualise the scenario: young wife walks in –

nurse lying on bed – husband breathless – it had all the ingredients of a compromising situation.

With my pulse racing I leapt off the bed, forced my feet into my laced-up shoes, then as I hastily adjusted my uniform I called out, 'It's all right, Mr Bowman, I feel a lot better now. I'll come in the kitchen for that cup of tea.'

I just managed to sidle into the kitchen as his wife was hanging up her coat in the hallway.

Chapter Two

'Oh girl, you looking terrible, what happen with your face?' said Sarah.

I slumped into an armchair in the nurses' sitting room. One eye was closing and the bump on my forehead, like a bookie's wallet, increasing by the minute.

As I explained what had happened and my timely escape from Mr Bowman's, Sarah rocked with laughter, and before long I was joining in.

Although Sarah and I had worked together on two wards at the hospital, we only became friends when we met up later as district nurses.

'My bike's had it. It's buckled to bits. I'll have to get a replacement.'

'Take a look at your stockings, kid, before you think about your bike. You know what happen if Miss Wright see them at lunch. You never hear the end of it.'

The nurses' home housed about twenty nurses and midwives, with the Superintendent keeping a watchful eye and pontificating over *her girls*. It soon dawned on me that I had exchanged one shackle for another. Here we were, qualified nurses and trainee district nurses, not one of us under twenty-two, yet still subjected to a matriarchal establishment.

I automatically reached for the needle and thread that would be on the coffee table at my elbow. No room was complete without a reel of black cotton and a needle. With the exception of the lavatory, all rooms had to have a repair kit. This was to silence any nurse from proffering the excuse that she didn't have the means to repair a ladder. I stared down in dismay at the mass of tangled threads that once resembled stockings. It reminded me of a piece of discarded weaving I had in my work box, all weft and no weave. Panic set in.

'Sarah, I can't repair these, there's more leg than stocking.'

'Take them off then,' she whispered, as one or two staff started to stroll into the sitting room.

I lowered my voice. 'It's OK for you being black, you'd probably get away with it. My legs would stand out like a couple of white flag poles.'

Sarah started to laugh.

'It's not funny, what can I do? Miss Wright will be furious.'

It was a disgrace to be seen with a ladder in the stocking; it was an indecent act to have naked legs.

'Listen, Monika, I have an idea. I have a large tin of black boot polish in my room.'

From the knees down she coated my legs in black polish. I looked in despair at my mottled legs.

'I'll never get away with it, I've seen better legs on a piebald horse.'

'Of course you will, I'll make them look more authentic,' she said, trying to stifle her amusement. She took a black eyebrow pencil from her dressing table and began to draw a wobbly line from the heel to behind the knee. This practice is not recommended to try on someone who is ticklish.

Nervously I made my way to the dining room. The immense oak refectory table imparted a solemnity to the occasion, whilst the high-backed chairs, heavy silver-plated cutlery and individual napkin rings, especially when we were working in a deprived area, seemed ostentatious. I snatched my napkin and slid into a chair next to Ian Newton, a new Queen's student. My colleagues were alarmed at my face and its battered appearance and did not bother to look at my legs. Miss Wright sat opposite. She looked across at me, frowned and stood up.

With hands raised and in a sweeping arc she gestured for silence, waiting for the murmurs of conversation to cease. With eyes closed, bowed head, she said Grace. Then came her customary speech.

'Now before we commence lunch and for the benefit of Mr Newton,' she began, 'I would just like to say that I do not allow my staff to "talk shop" at the dining table. This is not only *your* home, it also happens to be *my* home, the staff are *my* family. You may of course feel free to debate anything you wish, with the exception of two things, religion and politics.'

'That just about leaves the weather and sex,' whispered one of the nurses to her friend. Those within earshot sniggered.

There was a sudden outburst. Miss Wright bellowed, 'Mr Newton, how long have you been called Gertrude?'

'I don't understand, Miss Wright.'

'Your ring,' she indicated sharply.

Mr Newton fingered his recently acquired wedding ring, bewildered.

'Your *napkin* ring,' she thundered.

He had picked up Miss Wright's solid

silver napkin ring engraved with her name and family crest. Ian started to apologise; he was visibly shaking as he tried to pass the Superintendent her ring.

'I am sorry, here it is.'

In an instant it was heard spiralling on the parquet flooring. He lunged towards the circling object like a dog with a Frisbee, knocking the gravy boat with his shoulder. The china container wobbled ... toppled ... then spewed out its contents. The diners opposite, including 'Gertrude', were spattered with the hot brown gelatinous substance. I felt Ian's arm brush against my leg in an effort to retrieve the ring. He appeared from under the damask tablecloth, triumphantly holding aloft the shining object as though it were Excalibur.

'Mr Newton,' Miss Wright shrieked, 'look at the state of your uniform, you have only had it on one morning.' His white twill jacket with epaulettes that, until now, had been Persil white, now had a long black stain the length of his arm. He started to stammer nervously.

'I've n–no idea what it is, or where it has c–c–ome from!'

'I have, Mr Newton. It is boot polish, Mr Newton, boot polish.' She spoke slowly, deliberately emphasising her end consonants. 'One of my staff has the temerity to sit among us improperly dressed without stockings on. That nurse will see me in my office after lunch. Mr Newton, this is not a day I am likely to forget. Neither, I suspect, will you. Considering this is your first day here, you have certainly managed to leave your mark,' she said, mopping off the gravy stains from her once immaculate navy and white uniform.

It was not a day I would forget either. Later in the office, I was harangued as to how I had brought disgrace to the 'Queens' and humiliated a new member of staff.

I suggested to Sarah that perhaps it was time to spread our wings and look for a flat and share expenses.

We wasted no time and started to look on the shop notice boards. What I read brought me sharply into focus with what was then called the colour bar.

Notices were blatant. Most in large bold letters: **NO BLACKS/NO COLOUREDS /BLACKS NOT WELCOME.** The Race Relations Board had not yet been set up for support or advice. This was during the tyrannical era of Peter Rachman, the London landlord who exploited and intimidated his tenants. Despite being an immigrant from Poland, he had very little empathy for others. He would buy up large quantities of property, mostly slums, and let them out to West Indians and charge them excessive rents.

Many West Indian immigrants thought that they had come home to the mother country, only to find that mother wasn't exactly holding out her arms to welcome them. Black people found it virtually impossible to find accommodation. When they did, they were squeezed into tiny flats or rooms, some in terrible condition. When tenants were unable to pay, Rachman would send out his bully boys to recover the rent.

Ronnie Kray, the notorious East End gangster, took an interest in Rachman's empire-building activities and forced him to pay protection money. It is hard to believe anyone foolish enough to pay the Kray brothers with a cheque that would bounce, but apparently this is what he tried to do. Ronnie Kray sent his men to sort out Rachman's boys. Rachman was quick to size up the situation; and a gaming club in Knightsbridge that he owned suddenly changed its ownership.

During the Profumo affair Rachman's name hit the headlines when it was revealed that Mandy Rice-Davies was one of Peter Rachman's mistresses and that it was he who owned the house where Christine Keeler and Mandy ran their call girl operation. His name has now entered the *Oxford Dictionary*. 'Rachmanism' was coined to describe unscrupulous landlords who exploit and intimidate tenants.

We looked at the adverts and made a note of the few that didn't stipulate skin colour. Once we started knocking on doors, I was shocked how brazen people could be. White landlords would shout obscenities, look me straight in the eye, totally ignoring Sarah and yell, 'I'll take the white one, but I'm not taking the nigger!'

Their hostility and relentless discrimination filled me with a deep sense of shame. Some refused to speak. Some swore at us. Some slammed the doors in our faces.

'Why don't we try separately?' said Sarah.

'As long as the property is clean, respectable, reasonable rent, we'll take it then, regardless of the owner's nationality or race, agreed?' I suggested.

'Agreed,' said Sarah.

For a white person to find accommodation with a white landlord was fairly easy. The same for Sarah, she had no difficulty in securing rooms or a flat with a black landlord. As soon as Sarah mentioned her friend was a white nurse, or I said my flat mate would be a black midwife, they became overtly abusive. Black or white, I discovered prejudice was just the same. Occasionally owners put on superficial smiles to appear sympathetic, then the accommodation offered would be minuscule, uninhabitable or for an exorbitant rent.

I returned dejected to the nurses' home.

Helen Shapiro didn't help as she belted out *'Walking back to happiness'*, it failed to lift my mood.

Sarah arrived home much later, quite excited,

'Mik, I've found us a place. It's not exactly a flat, but it's clean. It's in a respectable area. In a quiet little road.'

'Slow down, Sarah,' her voice was soaring higher with excitement, 'it's not one of those converted garages we heard about, is it?'

'Girl, you think I'm crazy? Course not. It's in a large house.'

'Yes, and...' I said, waiting for the crunch.

'Well ... it has a large double room with twin beds, dining table and chairs ... it's all very clean.'

'Kitchen?' I asked.

Sarah started to mutter until she was barely audible, 'We have to share the kitchen.' Then loudly, 'But then, kid, we don't mind that. If they happy – we happy.'

'With *how many* are we going to be happy?' I asked.

'What? Oh, um, three or four, I think.'

'And bathroom?'

'Yeah, about the same.'

The large Victorian property had double bay windows and was tucked away in a pleasant cul de sac in East Dulwich. The owner, a Greek-Cypriot, was a small plump lady, dressed entirely in black mourning clothes.

With a practised smile, she explained that the accommodation was a double bed-sitter and that we could use the kitchen and bathroom, but we would have to share them with five other tenants.

It turned out to be very clean – very basic – very cold. It had two single beds, a small table, two wooden kitchen chairs, and puce linoleum.

We moved in a few days before Christmas, added a few Christmas decorations and personal knick-knacks in an effort to kid ourselves it was homely.

Christmas morning and we were both working. Sarah got up at half past six to discover that not only had we run out of gas, we hadn't the correct coins for the meter.

'This is ridiculous, Sarah, we can't go out in this freezing weather without so much as a cup of tea, especially on Christmas morning. This is as bad as when they offered us mince and mashed potatoes on Christmas Day for lunch at the hospital.'

'Yes, I remember. What a cheek,' said Sarah. 'We were told we would have to wait for the Nurses' Annual Christmas Dinner at the end of January.'

'Sarah, isn't there anyone about that we could ask for change?'

'There's no one up yet, and I've looked in the street. You can't expect anyone to be up and about this early.'

'This is terrible, talk about Christmas Day in the workhouse.'

Just then I heard the familiar drone of a milk float. I ran downstairs in my dressing gown into the street. I could just make out the outline and ran to meet it.

'Do you have any change for the meter?'

'Now 'old on, let's 'ave a butcher's.' The milkman delved into his back pocket and brought out some silver coins.

'Phew! Thanks, you've made our Christmas,' I said.

'Take these, love, and 'ave a good Christmas,' he said. He leaned over the float and took a pint of Jersey milk with its thick golden band of cream, and half a dozen eggs.

'That's wonderful, thanks,' I said, and kissed him on the cheek. He blushed like a schoolboy.

'Crikey, and that's wivout the mistletoe. Better not tell the missus,' he said. 'She reckons I gets all sorts of perks at Christmas – apart from tips. Mind you,' he tapped the side of his nose and winked, 'there are some women what don't always offer to pay wiv money at the end of the week, you know. I keep telling 'er there's only one person what would put up with my cold feet.' He grinned. 'She's getting worried now. She reckons there's somefink fishy going on, cos

I keeps forgetting to take me socks off when we goes to bed.'

We put a clean cloth on the table and Sarah added a miniature ornamental Christmas tree as a centrepiece. It stood all of five inches. We spread out our Christmas fare, two bowls of cornflakes with the cream from the milk. Propped up in small wine glasses were two boiled eggs.

'Christmas day in the workhouse, eh?' said Sarah, smiling as she buttered a piece of toast.

'Not now,' I said, pouring out a second cup of tea. It would have been luxury to have relaxed that Christmas morning and imbibed a few sherries and eaten hot mince pies.

I was mulling over this idea, when Sarah said suddenly, 'Here, I thought you were supposed to be covering for John Nicholson and his bladder daddies?'

'Oh God, I forgot I was standing in for the male nurse over Christmas.' I grabbed a piece of toast and got up from the table.

As well as bladder washouts, John had several elderly and disabled diabetics on his list. Until I had given them their insulin injections, they would not be able to have their breakfasts. Still munching toast, I glanced at my additional list and sped off on my bike.

Four injections later, I was on my way to Mr Sarkel. John had already briefed me of the cultural and religious observations and taboos regarding this patient.

Mr Sarkel had a catheter in his bladder and needed regular bladder washouts.

'Under no circumstances, Monika, must you show a square inch of flesh, especially in front of any of the ladies.' I assured him I would be very careful and very discreet.

I ascended the magnificent ornate spiral staircase and entered Mr Sarkel's room. The patient was sitting on a pink velvet tub-type seat surrounded by ladies of all ages. They were all sitting quietly. I smiled and greeted him, he did not reply. He wore a loose fitting Indian garment, a lungi wrapped around his waist. This made it easier to perform the washout with the minimum of fuss. I washed my hands and proceeded to lay out my equipment. Then very carefully I raised his lower clothing and discreetly attached the huge nozzle of the stainless steel syringe to the catheter.

Deftly I delved beneath his skirt-like attire, working mainly in darkness and silence. The only sound that could be heard was the gentle whooshing of the plunger from the syringe, followed by a loud cascading of fluid as it flushed into the enamel bucket.

I couldn't help noticing that where Mr Sarkel's legs should have been, there were two rounded stumps.

After I had finished I said goodbye. No one spoke. I smiled and left the room. I presumed that the lack of response was because neither the old gentleman nor any of the ladies could understand or speak English.

I reached the bottom of the stairs. Mr Sarkel's son was smartly dressed in a dark pin-striped suit. He was waiting to offer me a cup of tea. I tried to make polite conversation.

'I was sorry to see that your father has had to have both legs amputated,' I started.

'What are you talking about?' he said indignantly. 'He has some difficulty with mobility, but he has certainly *not* had his legs chopped off. Whatever gave you that idea?'

'I noticed when I went to give your father his bladder washout, he had what I thought looked like two stumps,' I said hesitantly. I was beginning to feel uncomfortably hot.

'If you did not see my father's legs, there would be a very good reason for it. By the way, did you notice the Ganesh?'

Ganesh? Whatever was a Ganesh? John spoke to me about certain taboos. There was no mention of this.

'I am sorry. I don't understand. What do you mean, Ganesh?'

'Did you notice a large brass elephant?' he said curtly.

'Well, yes ... now you come to mention it

... I did notice an elephant. I think your father was looking at it when I went in.'

'Precisely. You entered my father's room. You raised his lungi. You undertook your personal tasks. Do you realise, this was done at a time when my father was *trying to think of more holy matters?* At a time when his legs would have been underneath him.'

His tone indicated that he, like Queen Victoria, 'was not amused'.

'My father had his legs underneath him,' he continued, 'because he was *praying.*'

The Ganesh was a Hindu god. I could not have offended more. I had committed what today could be called 'a Rushdie' – I had blasphemed.

Chapter Three

Snow had fallen steadily throughout the night and had laid a virginal canopy over London. In the winter Sarah felt the cold much more intensely than me and had to allow herself extra time to get ready for work. For Sarah the onset of snow meant piling on numerous woolly garments under her uniform and several more on top. Gloves would go inside mittens, socks on top of socks, on top of stockings. Finally the ritual swathing of the head, using a scarf that could have belonged to the dancer Isadora Duncan.

As I waited downstairs for Sarah, the unmistakable aroma of bread baking rekindled childhood memories of Saturday morning pictures and Bourne's Baker's shop in Gillingham. For a halfpenny, I could buy a bread roll, hot from the oven, to eat in the Odeon cinema. Like a mouse, I would pick away at the crust until I had made a little tunnel and would savour its warm doughy contents.

My thoughts were interrupted with the kitchen door opening. Nana, a rotund lady enveloped in black, held out a small flat biscuit.

'You eat?' she said.

I thanked her and smiled. It was spicy and chewy.

'You like more?' asked the landlady.

I nodded. She offered two bags of bread pats.

'For your friend also.'

I thanked her again. We worked for a pittance and any offerings of food were always acceptable.

My thoughts drifted back to when we were training in hospital. Community nurses missed out on the usual hospital perks, left-over food from the wards and the inevitable conveyer belt of Black Magic chocolates.

Hospital life tended to skew the patients'

38

perception of the district nurse. Even though they had seen us use a syringe, draw up morphine, remove sutures, metal clips and drainage tubes, some would still pose the question, 'Haven't you ever wanted to work in a hospital or train to be a *real* nurse?'

I cannot imagine a patient challenging a GP in the same way.

One remarked, 'My daughter is far more qualified than you, she has all her Red Cross certificates.'

At home, naturally the patient is boss, the nurse the guest. Some patients, on return home, would become very insular and demanding of our time and unable to visualise that we had other patients to visit.

When patients were on an open ward they could observe the nurses dashing about and could see for themselves when other patients' needs were greater. Often they had a front row view of real-life dramas. One minute they could be talking to the man in the next bed, only to find him collapsed the next.

There wasn't a resuscitation team that would arrive in response to a buzzer or phone call. It was a matter of all the staff on the ward ready to spring into action at any given emergency. One nurse would go for the oxygen. We didn't have the luxury of it piped in at the bedside as it is today. It meant clanking a heavy metal cylinder, on its inevitable squeaky trolley, with a cotton bag twirling around at the neck, which contained the mask and a spanner to open the valve.

This was a sufficient signal to the patients that a *Your Life in Their Hands* scene was about to commence. And for the patient who had been waiting for a bedpan for the last ten minutes, to give a strangulated vocal of, 'Nurse, NURSE, any chance of that bedpan? I don't think I can wait any longer, it's really urgent.'

No response ... by now the nurse was muttering to herself something on the lines of *No chance, matie, it's not as urgent as this.*

Another nurse would run for the resuscitation tray, leaving the staff nurse or sister to start the kiss of life ... or in my case the kiss of death, as very few responded when I did it.

Soon one of the doctors would arrive on the ward.

You could always tell the seniority of the medical staff by their stethoscope.

1. The medical student would already have it hanging from his ears.
2. The junior doctor would swing it like a pendulum.
3. The registrar would have it stuffed in his white coat pocket.
4. The consultant, who rarely wore a white coat, wouldn't have a clue where he had left his stethoscope and a shout would go up for one to be brought to him.

The junior nurse would be wrestling with the screens on wheels. The supermarkets must have used the same prototype so as to make sure the wheels work independently of each other and point in different directions.

If the screens took too long in arriving, and naturally they would always be placed at the wrong end of the ward, the audience might just catch a glimpse of the doctor plunging an injection directly into the heart.

All this was guaranteed to increase the flow of adrenalin, and that was just the staff and other patients.

'What is happening behind those screens?' whispered one of the patients.

Muffled voices and cries were heard, the snap of a glass file, the slap of a hand to raise an elusive vein.

The patient who urgently asked for a bedpan was literally sitting tight now. He had something far more demanding of his attention. This was better than television, it was the real thing. He would sooner crap in the bed than be excluded from the unfolding drama.

Certainly by now, with the medical students and the rest of the patients getting wind of the emergency, the drama was not short of actors.

How often have you visited someone in hospital, expecting that person to give you the omnibus version about his trip to the X-ray, only to find the entire visit was spent listening to the complete script of all the conversations and incidents that had taken place to other people, complete strangers, within the last twenty-four hours?

When a young male patient was admitted and required to be on complete bed rest, he would flex his muscles, anxious to reinforce that he was in his prime and more than a match for any of the other men on the ward.

'Nurse, I'd help you if I could lift that man but the doctor has told me not to get up.'

The nurses would reassure him that they could manage. His fragile ego was further traumatised when he watched two young nurses, all of five foot, lift a man the size of Pavarotti.

The longer the male patient was in hospital the more he was apt to become agitated. Who was it said that men think of sex every few seconds? Guaranteed first question to man in next bed: 'What sort of job you in then?'

You would think that men would allow themselves the pleasure of going into a resting mode, switch off, forget about work for a few days. No chance. Once they had bored the pants off anyone who would listen to them about the intricacies of different operations, their overriding topic was WORK. The male patient's burning question when he had an opportunity to speak to the consultant? 'When do you think I shall be fit to go back to work, doctor?'

Women reacted more stoically and took to being a patient with far more aplomb. Once in bed with clean sheets and fluffed up pillows they would lie back and think of Eng– No, they would rather lie back and think of ... nothing. Women did reflect on certain domestic chores. How wonderful it was *not* to have to do the washing, the cooking, the shopping, the ironing, or clean out the budgie. They were delighted to discover that a mere moan, loud sigh, faint touch of the buzzer, had the affect of catapulting a nurse to the bedside.

One conscientious woman, who worked from home, *was* obsessed with work and brought in a week's supply with her in a shopping bag, but this was unusual.

'I've got to finish this lot off before I go home,' she explained. She had brought in thousands of white buttons which she had to sew onto small cards. She was still sewing them on minutes before going to theatre.

One or two women, when first admitted to the ward, would start panicking at the thought of their spouses struggling to cook for themselves.

'It's been so long since my Fred put his nose in the kitchen, he thinks scrambled egg still comes out of a packet,' said one.

Once home again, the family slotted back into their familiar roles and routines. The man could now relax, forget about impressing the staff with his tough guy image and revert to having his every whim attended to.

Sarah appeared on the stairs.

'Good God, you look as though you are about to embark on one of Fuchs' Antarctic expeditions. It is Dulwich village this morning, isn't it?'

'Don't be giving me cheek, Mik. Let's get going.'

Once we stepped out into the street, there was an eerie silence. The news was bad, with police warnings of abandoned cars and the customary advice that only people whose journeys were essential should venture out. Herculean efforts would be needed to carry out our visits. We would have to go on foot. We groaned at the prospect. For both of us our first call meant a three-mile walk, for Sarah to Dulwich village and for me Forest Hill.

This prestigious area of Dulwich village was home to Anne Shelton, the popular wartime singer. Later it would aspire to having Margaret Thatcher as one of its residents. We often used to joke that the villagers, with their beckoning tradesmen's entrances, would recoil at the idea of allowing us over the threshold if they were aware of some of the insalubrious places that we frequented.

Among my visits that day would be the 'formidable feet', two pairs of them – the appendages of spinster sisters. I trudged in the savage snow and wailing wind, pausing only to catch my breath and exhale like a steamy kettle, on the steep hill near their home. I dreaded going there. They were always rude, always ungrateful.

Now this surely should not have been considered urgent, when trudging on foot in snow up to our knees. Already I had pleaded with the Superintendent not to send me there.

'These ladies are widely travelled with frequent flights abroad and luxury cruises. They are physically and mentally fit and a waste of valuable time and resources, in fact I can't understand why they couldn't easily wash each other's feet.'

'Ah...' she said, 'you have forgotten one very important factor. They give exceedingly well to the Queens. Now that the sisters are in their seventies, they feel that it is time that they had some return from their investment.'

At that time we were still partly a charity. The local authority contributed 98 per cent, but we had to find the rest for the upkeep of the nurses' homes. A situation we thought humiliating, and meant doing the annual round with a Queens collection box together with the regular run of jumble sales and bazaars. And there was worse. We were expected to charge for performing last offices. When a patient died it was our duty and, frequently we were told, a privilege to wash and lay out the body of the deceased. We were expected to put one arm around the grieving relative then hold out the other for a donation of two guineas. I confess not once did I ask for a penny. I had three excuses:

1. The relatives were too upset for me to ask for the money.
2. The undertaker had arrived and the family were busy with the funeral arrangements.
3. They didn't have sufficient money.

By now my feet were swollen and painful and my boots far too tight. This miserable state of affairs was caused by:

wet feet
  dry feet
    cold feet
      hot feet
        resulting in:
          red feet
            shiny feet
              itchy feet
                swollen feet
                  painful feet

I was stricken with the complaint dreaded by all district nurses ... *chilblains.*

I began to shiver. The sub-zero temperature chilled my bones and every joint ached. Too often I had boasted to other nurses of the benefits of working in the community, but at least the hospital offered certain basic comforts. What would I have given for a nice warm soak of my *own* feet that morning. My fingers could not feel the bell push. Hardly had my hand left the button when the door opened. It was the elder sister, Phoebe.

'Our pipes were frozen this morning and we hadn't any water for our feet,' she said with disdain.

The relief! Thank God, I hadn't got to wash those damned feet. I felt like a school girl excused maths on the last day of term.

'But my sister Harriet,' she continued, 'has been out into the garden and collected some snow. She has shovelled it into a large cast iron saucepan, lifted it on to the gas ring and put it on to boil, so that you could have sufficient warm water to attend to our feet.'

My head and heart pounded, a surge of anger shook my body and began to rise in my throat. Relief turned to rage. I found myself responding in a loud jerky fashion.

'If your sister – is fit enough – to go out into the garden – collect snow – she is fit enough – to do her own damn feet!'

47

The sister's face blanched, then turned crimson.

'What is your name?'

I didn't answer.

'I demand to know your name?' she yelled.

'It is just nurse to you.'

'I will report you to the authorities.'

At this I could hear Miss Wright's voice ringing in my ears, *they give exceedingly well*...

'Miss Mason, in all the time I have been coming to you not once have you asked or showed the slightest interest in my name.'

'I shall report you, I shall report you,' she chanted.

I was beyond caring what she did.

'Go on then, report me,' I heard myself say.

So what, it would only amount to a torrent of harsh words in the Super's office. The sisters would refuse to have me back again and that would be the end of that.

By the end of the week the snow had turned to slush and we were pedalling once more.

On the Friday, Sarah and I arranged to meet for coffee at the Tudor Tea Rooms. I could see at once that Sarah was upset. On her way to a patient she had been accosted by a bowler-hatted gentleman walking through the village. He had raised his voice and umbrella to her in a threatening manner.

'Clear off, get out of this village. Go back where you came from. This is an all white area. We do not want any blacks here.'

'I am a district nurse, I have patients in this village,' Sarah told him.

'I don't care who you are, you are not wanted in this village. This is an all-white area. Is that understood?'

Sarah was clearly shocked by the incident, then told me it was the second one in Court Lane. Last time, a woman had tried to push her off her bike and told her to go back to the jungle.

'You must report it to Miss Wright.'

'She can't do anything. What do you think she can do?'

'It's important she knows what is happening. Come on, kid, let's have a coffee and a plate of our usual. Your favourite waitress is on today,' I whispered. Sarah managed a weak grin. The lace-aproned, white-capped, napkin-draped arm came over to our table. Sarah started to smile.

The old-fashioned tea rooms were in the style of the 1930s and had become one of the most pleasurable places to unwind. A pseudo middle-class voice spoke.

'What would Modom like?'

'Can we have two teas please?' I asked.

'What would Modom like to eat, would Modom care for a selection of cakes?'

'Yes please,' I said. By now Sarah's head

49

was bent over her lap, her shoulders trembling. At first I thought she was sobbing, then I realised it was in an effort to stifle her amusement. The waitress, having written the order on her pad, made her way to the serving hatch to speak to the kitchen staff below. We waited in anticipation. A gravel-throated cockney voice boomed to the bowels of the basement. ''ere Lil, two teas and a plyte of kykes.'

We could no longer contain our amusement. What started as a giggle became an uncontrollable outburst bordering on the hysterical. It helped us both to relieve the tension of that week.

Sarah later told Miss Wright what had happened and was withdrawn from the village, unless accompanied. As for me, a torrent of harsh words? More like a tornado. Within a few days I was back at the sisters' house. This time when the door was opened it was Harriet, the younger sister. She stared straight through me, then turned her head and called down the hall to her sister, in a supercilious voice, 'It's all right, Phoebe, it is no one of any significance. It is *only* Nurse Nobody.'

Chapter Four

'A man just poked his tongue out at me on the stairs,' said Sarah.

'He couldn't have done, he must have been licking his lips.'

Sarah shook her head. 'Don't think so.'

'Forget it, Sarah, it's just ignorance.'

It was easy for me to be smug and try to pretend it hadn't happened. He wasn't being rude to me. I didn't have to put up with being slighted or treated with contempt. I was white and that was supposed to absolve me. I knew it had happened. I just didn't want to believe it. My attitude wouldn't ease the situation and probably gave out a signal to Sarah that I didn't care. To pretend it hadn't happened could discourage her from confiding her anger, and hurt. By ignoring it, I had allowed him to get away with it and to indulge his racial hatred. To be honest I didn't know what to do about it. I took the easy way out and hoped it would go away.

'I am expecting a delivery this week,' Sarah said, changing the subject.

'I thought you had a break from midwifery when you are doing your Queen's?' I put the *South London Press* down and looked up.

'Not that sort of delivery. I'm expecting a delivery of an electric sewing machine'.

'I didn't know you could sew.' There was a lot about Sarah that I didn't know.

'I've been sewing since I was ten. I used to help my sister Pinkie.' Sarah looked embarrassed and quickly gave an explanation. 'We always called her Pinkie because she wasn't as dark as the rest of the family. My family had a drapery store in Jamaica and they used to take in dressmaking orders. The first item Pinkie taught me how to make was a bra. I made all my own bras, which is just as well, kid – where would I find a size twenty-eight bust? Soon I was helping to make all the different sizes. We had all the local women coming through to try them on. I used to look at those women, Mik, with overflowing pendulous breasts like melons, trying on brassieres the size of yam sacks. I reckon each boob would weigh a bushel. Every night when I was a child I would pray to the Almighty *not* to give me any boobies. Night after night I prayed, *God, there must be loads of women out there who want big breasts, please don't give them to me.* The power of prayer, girl. He sure answered mine.'

He certainly had, she was as flat as a couple of beer mats.

'Fancy leaving my electric sewing machine outside. You would have thought someone would have taken it in for me,' she sighed.

The machine had arrived and, to our disgust, the parcel had been left out in the rain under the window ledge.

'Surely it was not too much trouble to take it in. The rain could have ruined it.'

We carried it in and examined the sodden package. The machine appeared unharmed.

Sarah connected it and set it up on the table. It worked without a hitch. Later she let me try my hand. I was hopeless. I could use a hand machine but an electric was too fast for me. The material was either gobbled up or I was chasing it as it leapt off the end of the table. Sarah soon had it mastered. The whirring of the wheel, the tapping of the bobbin, pulsated late into the night and soothed like a barcarolle.

Soon the man on the stairs was not only poking his tongue out, he was holding his nose as he passed. Sarah tried hard to ignore it.

I was alone when the landlady called. I went over to the wardrobe for the rent.

'Lady, you and friend have one week, then must go.'

'*What!* – Why?

'You spend too long in bathroom.' As she spoke she put her hand over her mouth as though concealing something and fidgeted nervously.

'Who said this?'

She whispered, 'Not me, Mr Grogan, Irish

man downstairs.'

What a trumped-up excuse. We were up, washed and dressed and on our way by 7.30 a.m. at the latest. The Irishman didn't even go to work.

Mrs Grogan had always been pleasant, in fact she had recently called in to speak to Sarah when her husband was at the pub. She was expecting a baby in six weeks. She was anxious that we didn't mention her visit to her husband. At first I thought she had come to offer an apology on behalf of her husband's rude behaviour. Teresa Grogan was looking for professional advice from Sarah because she was a qualified midwife. They discussed the recent pains that had disturbed her sleep. Sarah reassured her this was normal and a good sign, and that the baby was having a practice run.

Sarah tried to treat his insulting behaviour with indifference. I felt an uneasiness and anger at what had now become a daily occurrence and was concerned for Sarah. What had hurt Sarah, wounded us both.

But what had started as a rude gesture from an ignorant racist had now developed into a campaign to have us evicted. He had forced the landlady, herself an immigrant from Cyprus, to get rid of us, playing his wife's pregnancy as a sympathy card.

We had just seven days to search for somewhere else to live in what was a bigoted, racist environment. It was not surprising that tension, fear and anarchy was beginning to simmer in Brixton when this attitude was being meted out regularly to its inhabitants. Sometimes it was the small incident that on its own didn't amount to much. I noticed how some shop assistants would leave black people to be served last. Yes, I know that can happen to anyone, but not every time or every day.

Grogan had lit the touch paper and I was ready to explode. I didn't wait for Sarah to return to discuss it with her, I went downstairs and knocked at Grogan's door.

Grogan was intimidating, all twenty stone of him filled the doorway. His beer belly wobbling over his studded belt. I was mesmerised by the tattooed serpent on his chest rhythmically swaying as if summoned by a snake charmer.

'I'm busy, what do you want?' he said impatiently.

I started to speak; my mouth felt like sandpaper.

'I understand you have complained to the landlady that we spend too much time in the bathroom in the morning?'

''tis the nigger, not you, I hate them ... bloody foreigners.'

I was furious. 'How dare you. How *dare* you talk about my friend like that. Who do you think you are? As for foreigner, who's

55

the foreigner around here? My friend's got a British passport, which is more than you've got. What's more, *she* works for a living and contributes to society, not sponges off it like *some* people.'

He sneered. 'You bloody nigger lovers make me sick.'

'You'd soon feel sick in the night, if Teresa needed a midwife in a hurry. You wouldn't be worrying what colour she was then.'

'Huh,' he snorted, 'if 'twas dark, I'd never find her anyway.'

'Don't worry, Mr Grogan, we'll be out by the end of the week.'

I turned and stomped up the stairs.

'God, Sarah, I was so ... so angry, I could have hit old Grogan in that grog bag of his hanging from his belt.'

'What?' asked Sarah with a smirk.

'Beer belly then.'

'Thank God you didn't, girl, the size of him. One punch from him would be like an elephant crushing a grape. Teresa was telling me he used to wrestle with Mick McManus.'

'Crikey! I didn't know that. Good thing I came away when I did. He could have picked me up by the scruff and butted my head to mush.'

'It's no laughing matter really, Mik, we've only got seven days to find some place.'

'We may have a better chance this time.

We could try the ads in the paper.

'Some hope, girl, with them rents.'

We started flat hunting again; this time we went in uniform. The discrimination was still there, of course, but sometimes it was disguised.

'Sorry love, the room has just gone.'

'The room I've got is too small for two.'

'Can we have a look at it?'

'No not really, the couple haven't moved out yet.' And so it went on.

'I've got an idea,' said Sarah 'you carry on and I'll see you later.'

On my own, my luck seemed to be in. When I said I wanted to rent accommodation for two nurses I was greeted warmly, but as soon as I said my friend was from Jamaica the door was slammed in my face again.

Once again, I returned despondent. It was dark. Sarah was still out. I began to get anxious. Eventually she returned.

'Where have you been? I was beginning to think something had happened to you.'

'It happen to me all right, Mik. I've got a flat,' she said with excitement. 'I've been to see it. Girl, it's the best.'

'I seem to remember someone saying that last time.'

'Ah, wait now till you hear this. Two bedrooms, sitting room, kitchen and our *own* bathroom. It even has a little garden.'

'You're kidding. How did you find it?' I asked.

'I went to an estate agent. First he shook his head, then he remember.' She took a postcard out of her pocket.

FLAT TO LET
FOR TWO PROFESSIONAL PEOPLE
LADIES ONLY

We set off the following day to view it, Sarah chatting all the way. How clean it was. How nice the owner, Miss Harris was, the size of the rooms. I was pleased that it was Sarah who had found the flat, she certainly needed a morale booster.

The flat was more than I had dared hope for. A large semi built around the 1930s in an upmarket area had been converted into two flats, with the whole of the ground floor to let. The house was in a tree-lined road and situated in a convenient triangle linking three districts. Although the postal area was Peckham, it was only a short distance from the Cherry Tree at East Dulwich and a two-minute walk to the corner of the road to be in the Camberwell area.

'Can we afford it?' I whispered while we were being shown around.

Sarah nodded eagerly. She hesitated, and said quietly, 'Yes ... if we don't eat much.'

The rooms were spacious and tastefully

carpeted and furnished. To the left of the bay window was a modern Ferguson radiogram; the wood gleamed and reflected the subdued light of a lamp on the coffee table. A Lebus bookcase took my eye on the far side of the room with its glass sliding doors. Together with a club-shaped three-piece suite in a tasteful pink and beige moquette, the room looked clean, comfortable and inviting. If it meant budgeting, economising, cutting back on food or forgetting about food altogether and taking a handful of vitamin pills, then this was it ... this was home.

'I'll have this bedroom,' said Sarah, bouncing gently on the single bed. 'This will suit me real fine. I don't want much space. You can have the larger one. You need it with all your books.'

This sounded a bit odd from Sarah. I could put all my books in the sitting room. With her interest in dressmaking, Sarah had loads of clothes, all her materials and sewing machine to find room for. It came as a surprise that she should commandeer the smaller of the two bedrooms.

My bedroom was nearly twice the size of Sarah's, with French windows that opened out on to a pleasant view across the garden.

A couple of steps down from the rear of the hallway led into a lemon and silver-grey kitchen that still smelled of fresh paint. It was well equipped and large enough to have our meals with its generous breakfast bar. Sarah patted the bar wistfully. As we stood admiring it Miss Harris pulled at the handle of the door of a narrow cupboard. We were astonished to discover it lowered as an ironing board. After viewing the flat, the landlady took us upstairs to her comfortable apartment for a cup of tea.

'I am surprised that you didn't keep the ground floor flat for yourself, Miss Harris,' I said.

'Oh I did live on the ground floor, dear, until I had burglars. They came through the patio doors. It was dreadful. They ransacked the place and made a terrible mess downstairs. The window was only open a fraction, but it was enough for them to get their hands in and unlock the doors. The police said I was very fortunate to be away at the time. I was staying at my sister's that weekend. I tried to sleep down there afterwards but I had nightmares. So a friend helped me to transfer everything upstairs and I have never slept down there since. That sort of thing wouldn't worry you, dear, would it?'

'Oh no,' I said, shaking my head vigorously and endeavouring to sound convincing. I tried to catch Sarah's eye. For some reason she seemed engrossed in a picture on Miss Harris's wall.

'Had you heard that about the burglary before, Sarah?'

'Yes, um ... er ... Miss Harris was telling me something about it,' she said, with what I could swear was a slight grin on her face.

As soon as our colleagues heard about the flat, there were offers of pots, pans and dishes. We turned nothing down. To our amazement Miss Wright gave us a box of crockery and cutlery left over from one of her notorious 'In aid of the Queens' jumble sales'. We didn't care if the cups were odd and that nothing matched. This was a proper home. This was freedom.

'We could even invite a boyfriend round for the evening,' said Sarah. 'Perhaps I could invite Winston sometime?' she added, with a glint in her eye.

'Why not?' I said.

Her relationship with Winston ran hot and cold. I thought he was a bit bossy and not very friendly. She would talk to him on the phone, but was unsure of his true feelings.

'Perhaps if you invited him over, you could get to know him a bit better. I could always disappear for the evening.'

After we moved in, unpacked and rearranged furniture, we were exhausted and ready for bed. Although I was tired, I found it difficult to settle as it was the first night in a strange house. I was beginning to nod off when a flickering beam of light illuminated the room. It was too close to be the headlights of a car. My heart started to gather speed. I heard a gruff voice under my window. I froze. Then broke out in beads of sweat.

''ere, Bill,' a deep voice whispered, 'over 'ere. Come on quick.'

The beam of light lit up the dressing table and caught the reflection of the mirror, sending a cascade of light around the room. To say I was scared was an understatement: I was petrified. I thought about going for Sarah, then I remembered there was a telephone on the landing of the next floor. I made to get out of bed – but my body wouldn't move. My legs felt like tree trunks with the roots wound tightly around the bed springs. It took all my strength to lift my head off the pillow. I remembered learning about the connection of fear and adrenalin and knew about the body needing a fight or a flight.

I was rooted all right but I hadn't an ounce of energy for a fight. I heard the voice again.

'Bill, come through here,' the rasping voice called.

Another flash of light and the sound of my window rattling. It was a blustery night and I hoped it was only the wind. My heart stepped up a pace. If I couldn't move, I had to devise a different plan.

I decided to feign death, in the hope that a burglar would be frightened off, if he walked in and found a body laid out dead on the bed. I managed to slide the blankets on to the floor and cover my head, with the white sheet. I straightened my body and lay motionless.

I was conscious of my breathing and thought about actors that played dead and how difficult it must be to control their shallow respirations. I waited. Listened – nothing. I woke to the sun streaming through the window, bathed in sweat. Looking about the room I could see that it was untouched and exactly as I had left it. What a night! The blankets were still on the floor, so I hadn't dreamed it.

I got up and told Sarah, who looked worried. I dressed and went upstairs to tell Miss Harris. She started to giggle,

'That would be George, my neighbour. He would be calling Bill ... his cat. He was probably shining his torch to get him in.' She laughed heartily. Sarah joined in. I laughed, from sheer relief.

'You weren't the only one that was frightened last night, Mik. It must have been the cheese and crackers. I had a nightmare about Winston, I went to his house and when the door open, there was a large curtain across the room. Behind the curtain a woman hiding.'

The dream played on her mind all day. In the evening she rang Winston and decided to try to pin him down.

'We've been going together for two years now, man. When you think you talk about marriage, eh?'

'Oh, that ting,' he said.

That thing, what you mean, man, *that thing?* Is that all you can say?'

'I thought we was happy together, just leave tings alone, I say.'

Sarah put the phone down in disgust.

The next day, unannounced and clutching her *A to Z*, she set off to see him. She had found his address in the telephone directory. She located the house and knocked at the door.

Winston opened it halfway and peered at her.

'What *you* doing here?' he asked harshly. 'I told you my landlady don't like me have visitors.'

Before she had a chance to reply, a woman called from a room at the back of the house, 'Who that there, darling?'

'It only someone selling something, honey.' He quickly closed the door.

It took a while for her anger to subside. Then came disbelief at the betrayal. And questions, always questions, and the numerous *if onlys* which she tormented herself with. 'Why was I so stupid? Why didn't I suspect something before?'

After two years this had hit hard like a thunderbolt. Like the storm beating on a windowpane, her fists beat loudly on the table. Suddenly, her head bent, tears trickled down her face as gentle rain. Tears of humiliation of crushed emotions and hopes dashed.

'The trouble is, Mik, I loved him,' she sobbed. 'I'll tell you something,' she sniffed, 'don't ever have bad thoughts about me, I will eventually dream about them. Just think, two years, Mik, two whole years I've been going out with that ... that ... *worm*. Just wasting my time. Look at me, I'm thirty. It begin to look like I'll never get married and I shall always be a splinter.'

'You mean a spinster,' I said, trying not to smile. 'For goodness' sake, Sarah, *marriage*, what ever do you mean by *marriage?* You can't mention *marriage*... Don't you mean that ... that ... *ting?*'

Sarah scowled, then grinned and tossed a multicoloured slipper in my direction. A rainbow on the horizon.

Chapter Five

Miss Jarvis met me at Maidenhead station. She was a plump lady of about fifty and wore her head-hugging hair in a fringe that resembled a grey rubber swimming hat. Her navy top-coat was long, faded and worn.

Her 1934 Morris 10 car completed the thirties image.

Before I left London, my colleagues had tormented me with accounts of previous trainees having to do breech deliveries, minor surgery and suturing. A Rizla cigarette paper would have been more than adequate to record the extent of my knowledge of obstetrics at that time.

Back at the flat in Peckham we had often joked that we were 'out in the rural', since we had been excused daily reporting to base and were accepting patients by phone. But this was going to be the real thing. The village was about fifteen miles from Maidenhead so I braced myself for a rib-rattling ride to Meadowbridge.

'I usually request non-smokers,' said Agnes as she drove through as many potholes as she could find. 'You're not a smoker, I hope?'

'No, not really.' (Not this week, that was obvious.)

Hell, I hoped I could survive without the weed for seven days and seven nights. I found my mind wandering and working out how many hours in a week that I'd have to endure without a ciggy.

Instinctively my hand found its way to my pocket to comfort myself with my customary nicotinic tools. I could feel the remainder of a pack of Senior Service that I had opened on the train that morning, and the scratchy sand strip on the box of Swan Vesta matches. As the car jolted and jarred I grasped the matches firmly to quieten their military march on the bumpy ride.

The nurses shared a three-bedroomed cottage. It was stark and lacked comfort. Not for them, soft relaxing chairs to come home to. After a hard day, it was hard upright chairs without cushions. I sat on the bed in the guest room. The mattress felt more suited for a horse to lie on than a visitor.

The women were triple workers, which meant they practised district nursing, midwifery and health visiting. They really *did* nurse from the cradle to the grave.

Agnes took me into the front room, which was a clinic-cumoffice, to meet Mildred. The windows dripped steam to the tune of the metallic clatter of bowls and instruments. Peering through the mist, I could see that Mildred was removing a pair of scissors with long Cheatle forceps from the stainless steel steriliser.

'You're young,' said Mildred. 'How old are you?'

'Twenty-two.'

'Yes, like I said – young.' She glanced up from fishing for scalpels. She had the lithe look of an athlete. A five-mile sprint before breakfast looked well within her capabilities.

'We rise early in the morning, at half past five. It gives us time for our ablutions, prayers and breakfast, in that order, so as to be out by seven.'

Oh God, the way she said *ablutions*. I could see that this rural training was going to be run like an army camp. She must have seen me pale at the thought.

'I hope you didn't think this was going to be a rest cure or a country retreat. You have come here to work, my girl. In fact we look upon it as a little rest for ourselves, when we have the London girls come to stay, don't we, Agnes?'

The fringed head nodded agreement.

The steamy room was where the surgical, maternity and general bags were sterilised and prepared. It also housed their home loans department and consisted of a small cupboard with two wooden shelves. Rolls of red rubber sheeting were neatly stacked at one end of the shelf, liberally dusted with powder to prevent them from perishing. Staring at me with wizened faces and Pinocchio noses were Victorian china feeding mugs. A pink wicker commode nudged against an ancient brown canvas wheelchair. Two antiquated china bedpans were hardly recognisable as such, with their long pouring funnels. Surely they were the sort that had undergone active service in the Crimea?

Mildred was endeavouring to remove a

kidney dish when it slipped and plunged back into the bubbling cauldron, splashing and scalding her arm.

'Oh glory, that's the second time today,' she exclaimed.

Then with a galipot of water and bicarbonate of soda she made a moistened paste. On a length of lint she added the cold poultice to her arm, covering it with a cotton bandage.

After a cooked meal and when I had finished the washing up, I left with Agnes to do the evening run.

We set off in the car to check the postnatal mums. The midwife took their temperatures and checked that they and their babies were making good progress.

With her health visitor hat on she advised the mothers about feeding, peered into the babies' nappies and made copious notes about different coloured motions.

'You must allow time for both mother and baby to assess their needs. The mother's temperature can be normal in the morning, then leap up in the evening,' said Agnes.

Jenny Parker was our next call, a cheerful lady despite being a week overdue having her first baby. She was examined by the midwife. Alan, her husband, was reminded of the telephone number to ring when the baby was on its way.

He took a small red book from his back pocket. 'I'll just check, yes I have it here.'

'Sister Jarvis,' smiled Jenny, 'Alan has been writing lists and organising things like a military operation. He has even bought two boxes of candles in case the lights fuse at the crucial moment.'

'Don't forget then, any time you need me,' she said. We drove away, waving to the friendly couple.

'We'll more than likely get a call in the night for that one,' said Agnes.

There were two more calls to make, a young mother with disseminated sclerosis and an older gentleman with terminal cancer.

Brenda had two visits a day. The nurse helped to get her up in the morning and ready for bed at night. Together we washed Brenda and helped her into her night-dress. Malcolm, her husband, would put her to bed later, when he had finished on the farm. Her two young boys aged eight and ten shrieked and laughed as they chased each other in the small cottage and let off steam. It was difficult for the mother to exercise proper control when the children knew her limitations.

She had been a school teacher until she got disseminated sclerosis (more commonly referred to today as multiple sclerosis) and she continued teaching from her wheelchair for several years. Many of her pupils still called to see her regularly and left her chocolates or a potted plant.

We drove on to Mr Davis, a man in his seventies who was terminally ill with lung cancer. His wife had already attended to his personal care. Our visit was to give him his morphine injection and settle him for the night. Today a district, Macmillan, or Marie Curie nurse would visit and set up a syringe driver into the abdominal wall with a measured dosage of the drug. This would give continuous pain relief and avoid constant injections.

Ted Davis had been a greengrocer. While he was at school he had helped out on his father's market stall. Later he was able to get his own stall to manage. When his father died and left him some money he rented a shop. At the time when we visited him Davis' Greengrocers shops were a household name in the area.

'My sons run three of them.' He paused to get his breath and convulsed with a coughing fit. 'I've put managers into the others.'

He pointed to indicate that he needed oxygen and I handed him the mask. Ted had already had one lung removed, now the cancer had spread to the other one.

'Mr Davis, don't, *don't* light your cigarette with oxygen in the room,' said Agnes, getting agitated.

Ted quickly extinguished it into his over-flowing ashtray. He looked at me and shook his head.

'It's a silly habit, but it's too late to give up now. It's my only pleasure,' he said, coughing profusely, his lips turning from grey to purple. He clutched his handkerchief and expectorated copious fresh blood into it, then fell back onto his pillow with exhaustion and his eyes sank into his purple and putty coloured face.

'I've got three good boys,' he rasped as he gasped again for breath. 'Money's no good to you if you haven't got your health. The last garment I'll be wearing, nurse, won't have any pockets.'

We made him comfortable and went into another room to speak to his wife Mavis.

'How long has he got, sister?' asked Mavis.

'I'm afraid it will only be a day or two,' said Agnes and put her arm around her.

Mavis sobbed, and rested her head on Agnes's ample bosom, like a child seeking comfort.

'What will I do without him? I've always relied on him to do everything, I'm no good at handling money or paying bills.'

'Try not to worry, Mrs Davis, your sons will help you with all that,' said Agnes. 'We'll be in again in the morning.'

It was ten o'clock when we got back and we were glad to sit down with a hot beaker of Fry's cocoa and a piece of home-made Madeira cake. As soon as we started to relax there was a knock on the door. It was Alan Parker. Agnes spoke to him then went into the front room and re-appeared carrying a bedpan.

'Have you something to tie it on with?' she called out.

'Yes thanks.'

He pedalled off into the night with the unwrapped monstrosity on the back of his bike. It all seemed so natural out 'in the rural' but I couldn't see any man doing that in London whether it was dark or not. Not even today.

I said goodnight. I was desperate for my bed. The hard lumpy mattress in the guest room no longer presented a problem; by now a bundle of hay in a barn would have been just as welcome.

Just as I was drifting into oblivion, Agnes called out, 'Leave your uniform handy in case we have to go out to Mrs Parker in the night.'

'OK,' I called back.

I swear my eyes had only closed for a minute when there was a rap on my door.

'Hurry up, nurse, it's Mrs Parker. Her contractions are coming every two minutes.'

I hurriedly dressed and looked at my watch. It was half past one, but with the excitement of an imminent delivery, I was soon awake. The car stopped outside the Parkers' house in the quiet cul de sac. It was easy to distinguish in the darkness as it was the only one with the lights on. Then like Christmas in Regent Street, and as if they had received a signal, one by one the neighbours switched their lights on, until the whole street was lit up. The neighbours had obviously received a coded sign when Alan Parker arrived back with the bedpan.

Jenny Parker was well advanced in labour when we arrived. In between contractions she would look up at me and give a little grin of anticipation.

'I do hope I won't put you off having your own family,' she said. 'I'll try not to make too much fuss.'

When it came to fussing, it was different with Alan. He was in a right flap and kept asking when could he bring the boiling water in.

'I think you have been watching too many films, Alan,' said the midwife. 'I'll let you know when I need some help.'

With an unmistakable cry, Philip weighed in at seven pounds two ounces. Agnes had weighed him strung up in a small cotton hammock with a metal scale attached. She turned to me with a huge smile.

'It doesn't matter how many babies I deliver, nurse, I still get the same thrill as I did with the first.'

'Now you can help me, Alan,' said Agnes. 'Take this newspaper parcel, put it in the dustbin and *then* you can bring me in some hot water.'

He went off cheerfully with the parcel under his arm, glad to be able to do something to help.

We chatted to the mother, admired the baby and marvelled how soon he could suckle after delivery.

'Go and see what is keeping Mr Parker, nurse,' said Agnes.

I went downstairs into the kitchen. There was no sign of him. The back door was wide open so I ventured into the garden. It was just beginning to get light. The birds were waking to a new day and seemed to be adding their individual song in celebration of the new arrival.

I looked around the garden. Slumped by the side of the dustbin in the half-light and in a pool of blood was Alan Parker ... out cold. I ran upstairs. Not wanting to alarm Jenny, I beckoned for Agnes to come downstairs to help me.

'Mr Parker,' I whispered, 'he's unconscious in the garden. I think he may have fallen and hit his head, there's blood everywhere.' I was trying to remain calm.

She quickly followed me downstairs into the garden. My eyes were gradually becoming accustomed to the dim light and beside

Mr Parker I could now see the newspaper parcel, wide open with all its gory contents revealed.

Agnes bent over him and, to my astonishment, she began to slap him around the face. Taking a large glass of cold water from the kitchen she proceeded to pour it over his head. With a cough and a splutter his eyes opened.

'What am I doing here? Where's Jenny and the baby?'

'Get up, you silly man, get up. You've fainted, that's all. No wonder your name is Parker,' she went on. 'That's what happens when you open parcels that have nothing to do with you.'

He rose to his feet. 'I think I'd better get that hot water now.'

'Yes, and while you are at it, four cups of tea,' said Agnes.

'Coming up,' he said as he stumbled towards the kitchen.

We left the Parkers' at half past five, each clutching a bottle of home-made wine. We were home in time for our ablutions, prayers and breakfast. Agnes added a little prayer for baby Philip and his parents.

Wherever I went with either of the midwives, each would proudly point out the children they had delivered: 'That one's mine.' 'I delivered that little girl *and* her mother.'

In the short time that I had spent with Agnes and Mildred I could not help but admire their dedication to the job and their commitment to the village. They were well respected and very popular and were often asked to open fêtes and judge bonny baby shows. Mildred was kept busy in her spare time as secretary of the local Women's Institute.

The week passed too quickly and when it was time to leave I was surprised that I began to feel sad at the thought of returning to London. London seemed on another planet. I had learned a tremendous amount in a short time, and I had to admit I had enjoyed my stay in Meadowbridge.

Agnes dropped me off at the station. As I made my way to the platform I fumbled in my pocket for my return ticket. There, still in my pocket, were two familiar boxes. It was then that I realised something... I hadn't given a thought about a cigarette all week!

Chapter Six

The sitting room was covered in blue velvet. Sketch pad in hand, Sarah was discussing with her friend Venetia how she wanted the sleeves designed for her ball gown. The

77

Annual Hospital Ball promised to be a special evening as it was thought that Princess Margaret would be attending.

After a brief discussion, Sarah took the scissors and confidently cut the material. For anyone who has ever dabbled in dressmaking, it was incredible to watch. No paper pattern, no chalk marks, no pins. I held my breath and watched with envy as she cut away at the expensive material. She was so skilful, a born dressmaker. Friends would call with a flicker of an idea in their heads. In no time, the sketch was on the pad, the material cut out in minutes. The machine would purr, the garment would be finished in a couple of hours.

Sarah bought most of her materials at Brixton Market for a fraction of the usual price. It was also her haunt for unusual Caribbean foods.

For general food we undertook a monthly shopping expedition to a Peckham supermarket. This idea is fine when you can load it all into the boot of a car. Believe me, it was not such an easy operation using two bikes, especially when the supermarket was at the bottom of the hill from where we lived.

Bags ... we had bags all right. Bags on the front, bags on the back, bags hanging from the handlebars, even string bags dangling from a couple of fingers. It was a dangerous idea. It would have been easier to have sent two overloaded donkeys to negotiate Hyde Park Corner in the rush hour.

Once we had set off from the shop fully laden, it was then impossible to stop. On one occasion, I attempted to prop my bike on a wall to adjust a rear bag. The imbalanced weight of the groceries was too much. The bag on the handlebar swung precariously then tipped out the oranges, apples and grapefruit and hurled them to the ground. The gradient was such that they bounced and chased each other like lottery balls to see which ones could line up at the bottom of the hill first.

I had no choice, I had to leave them; to try and rescue them would have created even more problems.

We shopped on pay day and took with us meticulous lists. We had to make quite sure that we had sufficient food to last us for the month. Menus were drafted for British food one week, West Indian the next. All very commendable except that once we returned home with the goods temptation would overcome us. Surrounded by this vast stockpile, I have to say it ... we were weak willed and totally devoid of that basic of all commodities, common sense.

Once home, we disgraced ourselves by pigging out on all different combinations of foods, piling our plates up, with a promise we would cut back next week. The problem was the following week we were just as stupid. By the third week with the cupboard and the fridge thinning out, we had to take a strong line and ration our supplies. By the fourth week, with all our good intentions, it was now too late. It would have to be beans and rice, cheese on toast, egg on toast, jam on toast, butter on toast, then dry toast ... ad nauseam. If pay day was not until the fifth week, we would be looking at eating the string and the paper bags.

The crazy thing was that when we did finally get paid, we were so hungry the feast and famine situation would start all over again.

On my return from Berkshire, Vernon was on the scene. Vernon was five years younger than Sarah, and worked as a clerk in a shipping office. He was a shy, likeable lad from Trinidad. We resolved to alter our eating habits as now we often had to stretch the meal to cater for Vernon.

'Mik, there's more meat on a skinny goat than on Vernon,' said Sarah.

He certainly always looked under-nourished, we had got to feed him.

'To be fair, Sarah, he never comes empty handed. He's brought a bottle of wine and some fruit already,' I said.

'But this week, girl, he bring flowers. We can't eat *them*.'

'Yes, well ... he's getting romantic now, isn't he?'

'He can start getting romantic without flowers then.'

It was difficult, in the circumstances. Flowers were literally not edible.

It was about this time that Sarah suddenly developed her allergy to plants and flowers.

I started to get ready for work and when I checked my list for the day, I noticed that there was a new patient, a man of ninety-two years.

The message read: *Mr Ripley 92 years. Mersalyl injection. Would nurse please go in the afternoon as Mr Ripley works in the morning.*

'Sarah, take a look at this. Ninety-two, that can't be right, they must mean sixty-two.'

'He couldn't still be working at that age, surely?'

Mr Ripley had the physique of a farmer, with broad shoulders, large hands and ruddy complexion. He lived with his wife in a prefab, one of the war-time properties supposed to be temporary accommodation to house the homeless, especially those who had lost their homes in the Blitz. They were single-storey, insulated and constructed from an asbestos material. Some people had been offered alternative accommodation and had turned it down, having grown fond of the 'prefab'. They were noted to be warm in the winter and cool in the summer.

He stood tall at the gate, with his rolled-up shirt sleeves and detachable collar flapping at one end. I followed him into the house.

'Is that right you are still working?' I asked him hesitantly.

'That's right, I am the oldest working man in London,' he said, knocking the ash out of his pipe and sticking his chest out as he spoke. 'I've got a newspaper stand on the Old Kent Road.'

The injection I was about to give him was a powerful diuretic, guaranteed to have him passing pints of water in no time. I was curious to know how he would be able to keep control of his bladder when he was out in the street selling newspapers.

'Easy, mate. I just parks me stall outside the pub then I nips round the back to the kazi. 'ere, nurse, there's the wife now, coming up the road with the shopping.'

He put his head out of the window and called to her.

'Come on, Ada, move yer bloody self, the nurse is 'ere. Look at 'er. Tut, she's only eighty-nine and there she is dragging 'erself up the 'ill.'

He leaned out of the window and shouted again.

'Put a move on, can't yer? Nurse ain't got all day.'

His wife arrived carrying two heavy shopping bags.

'Have you seen those new shopping trolleys?' I started to ask her.

'Cor blimey, gal, don't tell 'er that, make 'er lazier than ever,' he said.

A couple of weeks later I was watching the quiz programme *Double Your Money*, featuring Hughie Green, the Canadian compère.

'Turn the telly up a bit, Vernon. How old did that man say he was?' I asked.

'Ninety-three,' said Vernon.

'Yes that's right,' the contestant said. 'I'm ninety-three, Hughie.'

'Well that's wunnerful. Did you hear that, folks? Charlie here is NINETY-THREE. Let's give him a give him a big round of applause.'

Whilst the audience was still clapping the old man whispered something in Hughie Green's ear.

'What's that?' said Hughie. 'And you are still working? Wait a moment, folks. Did you all hear that?' The man whispered again to Hughie. 'Charlie here says he holds the record for being the oldest working man in London. What's more, ladies and gentlemen, he says he is getting married in two weeks' time to a lady called Irene.' The audience clapped wildly.

'Oh dear, that's terrible,' I said.

'What do you mean,' began Sarah, then she remembered. 'Oh yes, your man in the prefab, he will be upset.'

Another cheer went up, as Charlie asked Hughie to be his best man.

'Sure, I'd be delighted,' said Hughie Green, grinning towards the camera. Charlie left the stage to a tumultuous roar and to the tune *Goodnight Irene*.

'Oh, that's done it, Mr Ripley will be so depressed. He was so sure he was the oldest working man in London,' I said.

'Depressed, I'll depress him, he's been a bugger to live with all week,' said Ada.

Mr Ripley was drawing noisily on an empty pipe, sulking in the corner of the room.

'I tell you, nurse, 'e ain't no ninety-free, 'e don't even look no ninety-free, niver,' he said.

'What about him getting married to this lady of seventy and inviting Hughie Green to be best man?' I asked him.

'A load of old bull if you ask me, publicity stunt. 'e don't look that age, besides I *know* I'm the oldest working man around 'ere.'

A week later Sarah pointed it out in one of the national newspapers, it was all a hoax on the part of the couple. Researchers had discovered that he was only in his seventies and Hughie Green had made a statement that he would *not* be going to the wedding.

I longed to see Mr Ripley's face and I didn't have long to wait as I was due to call the following day.

'There yer are, gal, what did I say? 'e weren't no ninety-free. I told yer I was the oldest working man in London,' he said, his red face beaming.

'What do you think, Mrs Ripley? I asked.

'Don't ask me, nurse, I'm fed up to the back teeth with the whole bloody story. I've 'ad an earful of it all week. 'e fair wears me out, 'e do. My daughter's coming up this week to do me shopping. It's 'ard on 'er, yer know. She 'as 'er own to do. After all, she's seventy.'

'What no bike again, nurse?' said Mr Ripley.

'In the repair shop again.'

'Not another puncture?'

'Afraid so.'

'Why don't you bring your bike round 'ere. I'd mend it for yer.'

His wife gave me a resigned look and shook her head. 'Fair wears me out, 'e do.'

When I collected my bike from the cycle repair shop the repair man had a message which he insisted on reading out.

'"You have got the weekend off, if you want to book the coach." The message is from Sarah.'

'Thank you very much,' I said.

'Well, that's good, 'en it?'

'Yes, it's very good. I can book the coach at the National Express at the agent's down the road.'

'Going 'ome, are we?'

'Yes, that's right.'

'You can always give me any messages, you know. I've nearly always got one of you nurses' bikes in each week.'

We took him at his word and from then on he was our courier. Sometimes it was quite basic: 'Sarah says she's bringing in fish and chips so don't start cooking,' to 'I have given Bob his Cytamen', pronounced *Sight a men*, but our man always said *Sitterman*. 'No need to call.'

When Miss Wright decided that it wasn't necessary for us to check in the office for our patients list and that we could telephone in, we felt a tremendous sense of freedom.

Now with our repair man passing on coded messages we kidded ourselves we were really 'out in the rural'.

I was going home to Kent for a few days and called in the local travel agent to book the coach. He lived over the top of the office, and seeing the uniform (an occupational hazard) he started to tell me that he was suffering from panic attacks and that he couldn't go out of the flat. Today we would probably call it agoraphobia.

'How do you manage,' he said, 'cycling around London? Aren't you frightened of the traffic?'

'There is so much to think about when I'm cycling, such as giving the right signal, making sure I spot the right road quickly enough, checking I'm not going the wrong way in a one way street, there's no time to think about how I feel until afterwards.'

'Perhaps that's what I could do with ... a bike.'

'Why not try it?' I said.

When I next called into his office, he opened a sliding door at the rear of the office to reveal a brand new drop-handled cycle in the hallway.

'What do you think of that?' he said. 'It works, I've cracked it, I can cycle to the post office, to the newsagent's, it's wonderful. You're dead right, once you get in a stream of traffic you just have to keep moving and you haven't time to think of anything. Do you know, nurse, I haven't watched television for a whole week now.'

'You mean you've been out on your bike every night?'

'No, The Picador Café, opposite. There was a fight going on in the club over the top. All of a sudden there was a crashing of glass and someone had smashed the window. My goodness what a view, there were naked women running all over the place. I had a ringside view from my window. It took them a week to repair it ... thank goodness.'

'I bet he hasn't told you he sat there all

night with his binoculars,' said his wife, coming into the office.

I cycled off to my next patient, amazed at what went on over what seemed to be an innocuous little café.

It reminded me of the teenage patient on the gynae ward who told me how she worked as a hostess in a clip joint. Being quite naïve at the time, I asked her to explain what that entailed.

'When a man comes into the club,' she said, 'as soon as he buys me a drink I have to look at his wallet and estimate, by the thickness of the wad of notes, how much money he has on him. It is my job to extract as much of his money as possible. My drinks will be non-alcoholic. Nevertheless, they are extremely expensive. I might ask for a gin and I'd be given water or lemonade.'

I listened, fascinated.

'He is on a dream, in the hope that there is something in it for him at the end of the night, but I don't do that sort of thing. Of course there are rooms for girls that do, they can earn extra money for it.'

When she said how much she earned, I was shocked.

'You could do it in your spare time.'

I didn't know whether to feel flattered or insulted.

One evening a man rang the nurses' quarters asking for me by name. It was the owner of the club, asking if any of the nurses wanted to earn some extra cash... No I didn't, although in my impecunious state, it was rather tempting.

I arrived at my next patient and found the door unlocked. This was quite common. Often I would have a message that the key would be under the mat or on a string in the letter box. Sometimes a key would be lowered on a long piece of string from an upstairs window.

I walked into the house calling out, 'It's the nurse.' There was no reply. It was a warm day and the window was open.

Across the narrow street a woman called over to me, 'Are you looking for me, nurse?'

'Mrs Wheeler?' I called back to her.

'That's right.'

'Can you come over here'?'

'What for?' she replied.

'For your injection,' I said.

'But why can't I have it over here, nurse?'

'No,' I said firmly, 'I would rather you came over here.' Thinking how awkward it would be to start fiddling about taking the equipment to the other house. There would be a syringe stored in surgical spirit in a jar, needles in another. The injection file would be on a tray with cotton wool swabs. I presumed she was having a cup of tea with a friend, on the other side of the road. So I dug my heels in.

'Mrs Wheeler, if you want me to give you the injection you must come over here.'

'But I don't want to go over there.'

'Why not?' I shouted across the street.

'Well, for a start, I don't even live there.'

I couldn't believe it. Whose house was I in? I had entered someone's house and had been shouting out of their window. I grabbed my bag to make a quick getaway, when a young red-haired man entered the room carrying a pile of washing under his arm.

'What the hell's going on? Who are you? What are you doing here?'

'I'm sorry, I'm in the wrong house.'

'I can see that. You had better skedaddle before I get you to iron my shirts as a penance,' he said with some amusement.

Occasionally there could be a mix-up between Camberwell Road and Camberwell New Road, as I discovered to my cost, early one morning.

I pushed the heavy, scruffy door open. It was like a large hall with iron bedsteads in rows and back to back. The room smelled like a urinal at the back of a seedy pub. I had accidentally walked into a doss house full of tramps and down-and-outs.

The men obviously did not appreciate an early morning call and, collectively, wasted no time in letting me know it. Many jeered and shouted, 'Bugger off'. And they were the *polite* ones.

Others were very, very angry and began to take pot-shots at me, one literally, others hurling any object at hand. A Gideon bible whizzed past my ear and then a container a man called his 'spisso', a pot used for peeing and spitting in. It landed at my feet, soaking my shoes and splattering my stockings.

This was obviously not a convenient time to pursue the man whose name was on my list. It didn't take me long to make my decision ... I legged it.

Chapter Seven

Miss Andrews was disorientated and had locked herself in the bedroom. No amount of persuasion would motivate her to open the door. In desperation I rang the police. It was essential that she had her insulin. It was possible that following on from her confused state she could lapse into unconsciousness.

I had met Tony, one of the local bobbies, before. He towered over my five foot frame and I saw his blond head duck to get in the front door. He was very helpful and managed to break the lock so that I could get into the room.

I went into the kitchen to collect the insulin and the necessary equipment, and Tony called out as he walked to the front door, 'Don't forget, nurse, any time you need me just give me a ring.'

I took the necessary equipment into the bedroom and looked around the room – it had happened again. The old lady had disappeared. She had *now* locked herself in the lavatory. What an idiot to take my eyes off her even for one second. I couldn't believe it.

There was an affinity between nurses and policemen. We would often find ourselves thrown together for a variety of reasons. The first time I met Tony, he was fighting sleep at two o'clock in the morning on a hospital ward. He told me it was of utmost importance that he stay awake in case there was a chance that the unconscious patient should rouse and say who her assailant was. I would creep in the side ward and have a cup of coffee with him.

Another time when a drunk had started attacking the staff in Casualty, Tony was sent over from the local nick.

Late night chats in Casualty often led to a romance in between dealing with drunks. Nurses and policemen had similar work patterns and similar responsibilities and both dealt with life and death situations. Both had the unpleasant task, too, of breaking bad news to relatives.

There were occasions when Tony and I seemed destined to be thrown together. A young man had come off his motor-bike at Goose Green in East Dulwich. Instinctively we both ran towards the accident to render first aid, and collided.

Out of the fog a man appeared, intent on pushing us aside and taking charge.

'Leave this to me, officer. I am a St John's First Aider, I know exactly what to do.'

Tony and I looked at each other with an air of resignation.

'We seem about as welcome as a bacon butty at a bar mitzvah,' said Tony. He shrugged his shoulders and we walked away.

There was nothing for it, I would have to ring the police again.

'Are you sure you don't want a pair of handcuffs,' Tony joked as he broke the lock. 'I think I had better stay a while to make sure this lady gets her injection, don't you? I do believe you could be doing this on purpose, nurse, and wasting police time. I'd better take down a few particulars, starting with your telephone number,' he said with a wink. 'Next time, *I'll ring you.*'

'I felt such a fool not to have kept an eye on her,' I said to Sarah.

''Cos you too busy, that's what, eyeing up

gorgeous policemen. I know Tony. You give him our number?'

'I thought he was joking until he took out his notebook.'

'If he rings, Mik, why not invite him to our Independence Day party?'

We were planning a small party to celebrate Jamaica gaining her independence. We had both been out scouring the market stalls and shops for calypso records, the most important one being the new calypso, *Independent Jamaica*. It had been on the radio and ringing in our ears all week, and was imported on a Caribbean label.

After days of searching Vernon brought in a small bag with a 45 vinyl record.

'Any of you girls happen to be interested in this little number?' he asked. He teased us for a bit, holding it out of our reach so that we couldn't read the label.

Sarah grabbed a chair, stood on it and snatched the record. She shrieked, 'Man you got it, you got it.' She lifted it out of the bag and looked at its sleeve. 'Yes, YES, it's *Independent Jamaica*.'

In seconds it was spinning on the turntable and we were singing and dancing to the rhythm.

Independence is good for the young and the old
also for me and you
Independence is great for the whole population

including your children too
And I believe that if we try our best
it will be a great success
So let us live in unity
for peace and prosperity...

At one point Vernon shouted, *'Let's swing it Daddy.'*

Then we shouted in unison, *'Independent Jamaica.'*

Like a lot of calypsos it didn't necessarily scan, but it was a lively rhythm and had an amusing verse referring to President Manley, mentioning that 'Buster' arrived late for the conference. His unpunctuality was on record, for posterity.

We made our way around the supermarket to buy food for the party *and* our monthly food shopping. We had split the list between us and arrived at the checkout with two bulging trolleys filled with everything from cans of beans to bottles of rum. Two women in the queue couldn't take their eyes off us. Within earshot one said, 'Take a look at that lot, Daisy. You can't tell me they've bought all that on a nurse's wages?'

'No,' said the other, 'I reckon that paper was right about them nurses going up the 'dilly selling their bodies.'

We practically threw the rest of the groceries at the checkout, so as to get out of the shop as quickly as we could. The conversation was a reference to an emotive article in one of the tabloids. It pointed out that several nurses were so hard up that they were regularly seen in Piccadilly in their uniforms. The article said they were obviously soliciting punters.

There was an element of truth in some of the story. We did go up to Piccadilly. In fact I went regularly and in uniform. The best days to go were Tuesdays and Thursdays. But the journalist had overlooked the real reason behind our appearing there so regularly. It was all to do with Henri, he wanted us. Not just the odd one or two, he was looking for at least a dozen a day. We were so keen we were prepared to contribute a little towards his expenses. Not a lot, about half a crown (about twelve and a half pence). We were instructed that we must be in uniform.

Henri owned a hairdressing salon in Piccadilly and he would invite nurses to have their hair done by his students for a nominal sum. After the students pummelled, pulled and prodded our heads, many with long manicured nails (and that was just the male students), our scalps felt devoid of every scrap of skin.

Often I fell asleep under the hair dryer and awoke to an assistant shaking me. It could be three or four hours before we could get out of the salon.

I had often waited around in Piccadilly, but

not as the newspaper suggested 'for business'. I had sometimes waited for a colleague so that we could go in together to the salon. I doubt if any one of us could afford the real price but eventually one of the professionals, maybe even Henri himself, would tidy up the tangled bird's nest that had at one time resembled hair and made it all worth the pain. We could then step out of the salon looking and feeling like duchesses.

One afternoon I was waiting for a friend when a woman in a full-length fur coat came up to me.

'What the bleeding hell do you think you are doing? I suppose you think you are trying to be clever,' she shouted, and started trying to push me off of the pavement into the gutter. 'Get off my bleeding pitch.' She gave me a final shove and I narrowly escaped falling under a bus on the busy city street.

Coming out of the salon, my friends and I, decided to go into a large restaurant for a coffee. As we sat drinking coffee I noticed the fur coated woman chatting up an older businessman. She stretched over to another table to pick up a sugar bowl and the single button flew off her coat to reveal an entire naked body. We watched in amazement at her indifference as to what had happened. The red-faced businessman left in a hurry. The woman, however, continued to slowly sip her coffee as though it was an everyday occurrence. Which I suppose it was really. Although not usually in such a public place.

When I arrived home, Sarah was doing her own hair in the kitchen. But, before she could do anything with it, she was applying some grease from a tin, before plunging her hair into hot metal tongs. These she had heating on a gas flame on the top burner. When the tongs were ready she would straighten her hair first, then curl it. It looked a highly dangerous operation to me, especially on short hair. She assured me that the grease would prevent the hair from getting burned.

As we got ready for the party, she told me why her hair was unmanageable and not proper African hair.

'It's all because of the slave owners in the past. They had sex with their slaves and their offspring inherited two opposing hair textures. My surname is Scottish and that would have been the slave owner's name, which the slaves and their children would have had to adopt.'

We put the music on to get in the mood as we greeted our guests. There was no sign of Tony so I busied myself playing the host and handed out plates of curried goat that I had help cook, with a mound of pink rice. After the meal, the wine and rum flowed and we all danced to reggae and calypso records. We took turns at attempting the limbo. I was hopeless at it and landed in a crumpled heap most of the time.

'Is that the twist, Mik? I think I know how that goes,' said Sarah. She invented her own version she called The Twistimbo, the twist ... limbo style. To rapturous applause.

We put on our special record that Vernon managed to find at the last minute. A huge cheer went up, with everyone shouting 'Independent Jamaica'. Suddenly there was a knock on the door and one of the lads looked out of the window.

'Stop, turn the volume down, it's a blue-bottle.'

'I've heard louder music than this at a funeral,' said his friend. 'It's only nine.'

'Anyone going to open the door? I'd better go,' said Sarah.

'Relax man, it's Mik's friend,' Sarah called out.

'She's in the kitchen Tony,' said Sarah.

'I'm sorry, Monika I can't stay, my duty has been changed. Are you free Monday evening? Perhaps you'd like to come with me to the Trocadera at the Elephant.'

'Yes, that would be fine,' I said.

'I've got my own transport, I'll pick you up at six thirty.'

'Mik, you are no nearer sorting out what you're wearing and you've had three days. I could have made you a new outfit in the time it has taken you to make up your mind.'

'I've decided now, it's the outfit I wanted to wear in the first place. The light green suit, with the pencil slim skirt and navy accessories.'

'Move yourself, he be here, girl, any minute. You won't find me opening no door, you'll have to get there, in your bra and pants. No, the pale pink lipstick it look fine,' echoed Sarah.

To my relief Sarah did let Tony in and gave him a cup of coffee, while I finished my make-up.

Tony looked just as handsome out of uniform; he wore a black leather jacket that looked very expensive. He gave me a puzzled look but said nothing as we left the house. When I saw the 'transport', I wished I had worn my black trews, tapered trousers cropped below the knee. This fashion is back as pedal pushers or clam diggers today.

Tony beckoned me towards his gleaming Triumph motorbike. It was difficult to sit pillion with a straight skirt despite the kick pleat at the back. It was not the occasion for sophistication. I put my arms around his waist and gripped him firmly. This was my first time on the back of a motorbike and I listened intently to what he had to say about leaning to one side when negotiating the corners.

The skirt began to feel increasingly tight and I was worried that I might split the seam. To dismount and find I only had two halves to my skirt hanging from the waist band could be more than just a little embarrassing on my first date.

As we approached the red traffic light, I heaved a sigh and placed my feet on the ground and proceeded to hitch my skirt up above my knees. Fortunately I was under cover of darkness. The mini had not yet arrived. Other than on the beach or in a pair of shorts we would not have shown our knees.

The lights swiftly changed and I felt the seat slide under me.

'Hey! Tony, wait,' I called, but the roar of the engine and the noise of the other traffic was deafening. I had unceremoniously been dumped with a mile to walk back.

'What you doing back here, girl? Forgotten something? No, Mik, after all that fuss, what to wear, buy special makeup, then he up, rode off – left you there?'

'The worst thing is, he didn't even notice I was missing, I don't suppose he will even bother until he reaches the cinema at the Elephant and Castle.'

'Oh, come on, he's bound to notice with no big weight on the back.' She began to giggle. 'Sorry, Mik, but you give a real joke. What you going to do?'

'Nothing. What *can* I do? He probably thought I changed my mind and got off the bike and went home.'

Tony stood in the doorway,

'That's the shortest date I've ever had. What happened to you? Are you hurt? Did you fall off?'

I explained what had happened at the traffic lights. He roared with laughter.

'Do you want to give it another shot?' he asked.

I nodded and quickly disappeared to get changed.

'We may miss a bit of the first film, but we'll still be in time to see the main one.'

We arrived halfway through the first film. As the lights went up for the interval Tony groaned as he spotted three youths a couple of rows in front of us.

He whispered, 'I know one of those lads. I got him sent down. He's just come out of Rochester Borstal.'

One of the lads started shouting. He stood up and pointed at a girl a few rows in front and in a loud voice, ''ere, ain't that your girl darn there?'

The boy with grease-loaded hair sculptured in a quiff stood up to get a better look.

'Naaah.'

'What! Don't yer go wiv 'er no more?'

'Naaah.'

'Why's that then?'

There was a long pause ... then a gravel voice loud enough to be heard in the foyer, 'Naaah ... she wouldn't give me nuffink!'

You could have heard a solitary popcorn drop. I wished the lights would go out to hide my embarrassment. Hardly a conversation conducive to a first date.

Chapter Eight

It was that time of year when the GP surgeries were bursting at the seams. People were sitting clasping their soggy handkerchiefs, sniffing and sneezing, and the air was impregnated with the smell of Vick. That is, until Dr O'Leary strode in, having been called out for yet another patient with a heavy cold masquerading as flu.

'Now listen here, all youse folks sitting there sniffing in your handkerchief wid a cold. Have any of youse heard of a cure for the common cold? No, of course not. 'tis a rich man, so it is, that would have the answer. So go home and take two aspirins every four hours until it has gone. Now all of youse who tink you have the flu,' he shouted, 'what the hell are you doing here giving it to us all. You should be in your bed, so you should, keeping warm, taking aspirins and

103

hot milk with a generous measure of the good stuff. Those of you that are *really* ill, see me in my surgery. I can't be doing with any time wasters.'

One by one, they scattered. One little old lady beckoned him over.

'Dr O'Leary, I am feeling really ill,' she said quietly.

'Sure you are, me dear. Bless you, come on in and see me.'

Dr O'Leary was due to retire. Like most of the GPs at that time, he was a single-handed practitioner. His unorthodox method of clearing his waiting room was not a lesson in diplomacy.

At a more modern surgery Dr Cox, fresh from hospital, always seemed to be a young man in a hurry. A well-fed man, or as one patient was heard to remark, 'By God, I can tell *you* like your grub, doctor.'

He was a big man, with ego to match.

Every Friday afternoon, Mrs Benson had her injection for rheumatoid arthritis. When I called, her husband invited me in.

'You've just missed her. The ambulance has taken her away. It's been a madhouse here.'

'What's been happening?'

'I had to call out that young doctor, what do they call him? Dr Cox, that's right. Lena was taken bad, said she couldn't breathe, so I sent for the doctor. Took his time getting here. By the time he arrived, she was uncon-scious. He tried to revive her. Then he looked at me, shook his head and said, "I'll send for the ambulance, but I can't feel a pulse. I think it is all over, Jim," then he left. Two ambulance men came. One, a little man, kept saying, "Keep calm, don't panic." He was panicking more than anyone. When they tried to bring Lena down the stairs, the little fellow started to lose his grip. He was shouting, "It's no good, I can't hang on, I'm dropping her." With that he let her fall.

'She fell the full length of the stairs. The racket was awful, her body thumped on every step until she ended in a heap in the hallway. Suddenly she started to cough and then she came round. She opened her eyes, looked around and asked what all the fuss was about. It was a miracle – I know it sounds stupid, nurse, but if they hadn't dropped her, she wouldn't be alive now. She was a gonner.'

It was an amazing story. At first Mrs Ben-son protested and refused to go to hospital. Nevertheless the ambulance men took her in for a check-up. She was home three days later with no ill effects after her ordeal, except bruising – she was covered in bruises – a small price to pay.

When I called in at the surgery for a pre-scription, I heard that Dr Cox was back from his holiday in Spain. The same afternoon he had left Mrs Benson for dead, he had left for his holiday.

The door burst open. Dr Cox was in a terrible state, his face blanched and his body shaking.

'What's happened to you?' asked Dr James.

'You are not going to believe what I have just seen. I have seen the ghost of one of m-m-my patients,' he stuttered.

The receptionist started to giggle.

'It's no laughing matter. I said you wouldn't believe me, but it's true. Mrs Benson had collapsed and died, there were no vital signs. I more or less certified her dead two weeks ago. Sent her off to hospital as a BID.'

'So you have just seen her ghostly figure floating about,' said Dr James, struggling to contain himself.

'I know you think it's funny, but I tell you I saw her a few minutes ago.'

'Oh come on, Dr Cox,' I said, joining in. 'You surely don't believe in ghosts?'

'It's OK for you to laugh, nurse. I'm serious, I tell you I've just seen her.'

'What was she doing then?' asked Dr James, encouraging him.

'She was standing on a stool outside her house cleaning her windows. Then, as I passed by her house, she turned round and ... and waved to me. I put my foot down and drove as fast as I could to the surgery. I couldn't look back. It was too spooky. I know you don't believe me, but it is absolutely true.'

We could not hold back the laughter. Dr James had tears rolling down his face.

'I've had enough of this,' said Dr Cox and stormed into his office. A few minutes later he re-appeared. In his hand were Mrs Benson's notes.

'You rotten sods, you let me carry on, and you knew about her all the time.'

It was several minutes before all the laughter died down. Much longer than that before Dr Cox was allowed to forget his ghostly experience.

I quickly learned *not* to ask Dr Cox directions to a patient's house. He was so pompous and fancied himself as a lecturer. He would expect me to remember my physiology in order to locate the patient.

'The area you want is laid out like the intestine, nurse. Morland Road is your ascending colon. Hillmead your transverse and Sussex Walk your descending colon. Mr Briggs lives on your descending colon very near to your appendix, which would be Geneva Road.'

'I see, Dr Cox,' I said, much to his annoyance one day. 'So if I miss my turning and go under the railway bridge, I should find myself coming out of my rectum!'

When I was a student nurse in theatre, one of the local GPs had an excellent reputation as a diagnostician and would have made a marvellous lecturer. Whenever he sent a patient into our hospital with suspected gallstones, then that is what it would be. The surgeons had such confidence in his diagnosis they would ask the theatre staff to lay up a trolley for a cholecystectomy.

'How do you know it *will* be biliary calculi?' asked one of the medical students.

Many surgeons classified GPs as jacks of all trades. It was refreshing that this particular GP was held in such high regard.

'If the patient has been diagnosed by Dr Swartz, if he says it's gallstones, then gallstones it will be.'

One afternoon I called at a small shoe repair shop. I was about to hand over some shoes for heeling. The next thing I remember was looking up at a dusty light bulb and wondering where I was.

'Who are you?' asked a man with a continental accent. I told him.

'Have you got a doctor?'

'No, not yet.'

'Well, you have now.' A hand was thrust into mine. 'I am Doctor Swartz. Come now, Monika, I will take you home.'

For five days, I had a temperature over 100F. Dr Swartz visited every day.

'If you are no better tomorrow, I will have

you admitted to hospital with a kidney infection.' My temperature dropped the following day.

'You jammy thing, trust you to pass out two doors away from Dr Swartz's surgery. But it was a bit drastic just to get on his list,' said Sarah. 'His list is full he's not taking on any more new patients. By the way, Miss Wright sent you a present. Some grapes and a bottle of Lucozade.'

'Great, now I know I'm dying.'

A head popped round the door.

'Hallo there, how are you feeling?' asked Vernon. 'You had better be well enough for next Saturday.'

'Why, what's happening next Saturday?'

'I said there was no need for you to finish Mik's wedding outfit, Sarah – she will have forgotten about the wedding when she comes round,' said Vernon.

'Yes I remember now.'

Sarah was making me a summer dress and jacket. I toyed with the idea of buying a hat to match to go to my friend's wedding at Woolwich.

Two days before the event Sarah and I spent an amusing morning trying on all the hats in C & A. I looked at a lovely lemon tulle creation. I had really set my heart on it, when a French customer pulled a face and eyed me up and down then interrupted, 'Non, non, non, not wiz zer yellow 'air.'

I was mid blonde but she put me off altogether and I decided to forgo the hat and spend the money on having a false hairpiece woven into my own hair.

On the morning of the wedding, I arrived at the hair salon with my false piece. I spent a tedious morning having my hair washed and set and the false hair intertwined into my own in an intricate topknot. When it was finished it looked marvellous and, for me, very sophisticated.

I went by bus to the church. I kept peering at my reflection in the rain-dotted window. Just in time I noticed my landmark and made my way to the exit. A gentleman in a hurry pushed past, snatched up his umbrella from under the stairs and jumped off the bus.

Suddenly my hair was wrenched at the roots and my false piece lifted from its anchor. There, perched resplendent on top of the gentleman's umbrella, was my golden topknot. My hair flopped immediately and became a yellow helmet. I looked a mess. I would *have* to wear a hat now. With minutes to spare, the only shop I could see was Woolworth's. I dashed in, frantically searching for something suitable to match my lemon outfit. The only 'hat' was a black beret. Worn at a sexy angle I thought I might look seductive and sultry like Marlene Dietrich. The heavy rainfall compounded the problem.

Being wool, the beret started to shrink.

By the time I reached the church I looked a mess, *wiz my yellow 'air* sprouting in all directions. The hat had shrunk so much and was so tiny, it looked like the proverbial pimple on a duck's bum.

Chapter Nine

Regina, a friend of ours, was returning to Jamaica and there was to be a party in her honour at one of the clubs in Brixton. Sarah and Regina invited me to join them.

Outside we could hear the happy lively atmosphere with laughing, dancing and singing. We walked into the room to see about fifty people dancing and enjoying themselves to reggae music. Like musical statues, the music stopped. All stood still and stared despite my being accompanied by two black friends. Regina called out, 'It's OK, she's with us.'

The silence was probably about a minute, but felt much longer.

Occasionally, people had stared at me in the street when walking with a group of black friends and there had been the odd remark such as *nig-shit* from the white community.

This was different, it was soon forgotten.

The party continued and I joined in. Although I felt uneasy and nervous at the time, this was an isolated incident. You might think that I could now understand what it felt like for Sarah. I would never know, it was not possible for me to get inside the skin of a black person. Besides, I could always walk away from it all, if I wanted to.

Regularly white people were given priority and treated differently. I could hear the change of tone in the voice when addressing a black person. I could feel the air of resentment, the inner disquiet and restlessness. Although there was a large black community, they were still in the minority. They were conspicuous, to be stared at, and yet if it suited the white person, they could be invisible and ignored.

Many West Indian men had fought and given their lives in World War II, for this country.

It was to the West Indies again that Britain turned for help when the work force was depleted following the war. We invited them here. We advertised in their newspapers. The West Indians did not envisage hostility on their arrival. This was supposed to be their Mother Country.

Some newly arrived immigrants found that black strangers would approach them with an offer to straighten their hair or make their skin look lighter, in an effort to be socially accepted in an unfriendly country.

Over and over again like a broken record I would hear, *'Bloody blacks, come to our country take our men's jobs, go to the top of the queue and take our council houses.'*

They omitted to point out that the jobs tended to be the ones that no one else wanted, porters, bus drivers and railway guards. And the houses that they rented in London were often in the worst areas, once occupied by former immigrants, Jews, Italians and Irish, who fared little better when it came to being accepted by society. Once their circumstances improved they were able to move on to a better district and improved housing.

Ironic that this should be at a time when white women were taking themselves off to sunny Spain to laze in the Mediterranean sun to get as brown as possible.

Since then we have acquired sun beds and tanning sprays. We have had the Afro hair-style, and today movie stars and the cosmetic industry are placing an emphasis on making the lips of white women look larger and fuller, to the extent of injecting them with silicone gel.

When Sarah and I were doing our hospital training, there was a blind lady in her nineties who latched on to Sarah and would have no other. It was only Sarah that she wanted for bathing and washing her.

As Sarah started to get her ready for bed, Mrs Bond began to chat to her. I was at the next bed, so I overheard the conversation.

'It's not right, you know, them darkies coming over here taking our boys' jobs, taking our houses. They ought to go back where they came from. What do you think, nurse?'

'I hear a lot of people talk about that, Mrs Bond. Personally I don't know what to say about it,' she said.

Afterwards, I said to Sarah, 'Why do you put up with that? Why didn't you tell her you were black?'

'I don't need to,' she said. 'She's an old lady, she knows no different. If she could see me she would never say that to my face. She wouldn't want to hurt me. If I pointed it out to her that I was black, what good would it do? She would be very embarrassed. It would ruin the relationship that I have with her. I certainly don't want to upset her. To her everything is black.'

When Mrs Bond died, Sarah wept openly. She said she had lost a dear friend. And I learnt a valuable lesson in humility.

Sarah was away at Pinkie's so I decided to catch up on some correspondence. I was just on my second letter when the phone rang. I waited for the landlady to answer it. After five rings I went upstairs on the landing to take the call.

'Monika, it's Bill Gleeson, Lofty's friend. He gave me your telephone number and address. He said he didn't think you would mind if I contacted you.'

I paused for a few seconds, trying to remember who this was.

He continued, 'It is Monika, isn't it? You remember me, I'm the tall guy with black unruly hair and big feet.'

I smiled to myself at his description and the remark about his feet. Sarah would have straight away said, *Ah, Mik, you know what they say about big feet?*

'Yes, of course I remember you. We met at Lofty's twenty-first.'

'What are you doing tonight? I wondered if you fancied showing me the hot spots of Peckham?'

'I'm not sure what my plans are tonight,' I said, trying to stall him.

'Listen, forget your plans. Unless you say no in the next five seconds, I'll be there knocking on your door. OK?'

'All right. What time will you be round?'

'Give me two minutes, I'm at the bottom of your road in a call box.'

It was nine thirty in the morning and I was still in my dressing gown. I grabbed the first thing to catch my eye and dressed quickly. As I put my make-up on, I arched my eyebrows so quickly I had a permanent look of surprise on my face. A quick flick of the hair, squirt of perfume and he was at the door. I made some coffee while he talked.

'I've been trying to hold down a full-time job and write in the evenings,' he said. 'When I started to sell a lot of articles and stuff, I decided to give up my job at the bookshop and concentrate full time in the day. When I have any spare cash, I take off and enjoy myself. Of course it would be more fun to have someone to share it with.'

'What's happening about your writing today?' I asked.

'It's my day off,' he grinned.

'How about Brockwell Park? We can go by bus from here. We can take a picnic if you like,' I said.

'Fine, I'll help with the sandwiches.'

What Bill lacked in looks he certainly made up for in humour. He was a very easy person to talk to. Although we had only met each other in passing at Lofty's party, I immediately felt at ease with him.

We sat by the lake, and had our picnic. Bill chatted non-stop. He seemed lonely. He had lost both parents by the time he was seven and was living with his grandmother.

'How about Acker Bilk with me tonight?' he asked.

'Acker Bilk? That sounds a made-up name. I've never heard of him, you've just invented it,' I said.

'No, seriously, it's jazz.'

In the late fifties as a student in the hospital and not possessing a radio, I was ignorant about the music industry and missed out on current affairs as well. I had to ask my father when I went home whether the Korean War was still on.

We both enjoyed the concert and Bill took me home. He was living in Battersea so it was quite a trek for him to go back home again from Peckham.

With the change of social mores today, it would have probably have been the question, 'Aren't you going to invite me in for a cup of coffee?' and the ensuing bedroom scene. The pill had not yet arrived to emancipate women. Until then the majority of women and men used a tremendous amount of restraint. We were still using the persistent and powerful contraceptive that was swift and took less time than taking a pill, the word... NO!

Girls would often say *'It's against my religion'* or *'I'm saving myself for the right person'*. If the girl had a steady relationship and was courting, although she may not have realised it at the time, it was really the fear and stigma of becoming pregnant that dictated the terms.

Nurses knew that back street abortionists were rife and septic abortions took life. As nurses, we saw the whole sordid picture when young girls would try anything to abort the baby.

Most of the girls when dating boys would have ways of warning other girls if the fellow was too hot to handle. *'Watch him, he belongs to the WHC'* (the Wandering Hands Club).

It was a common expression for girls to say, *'I'll be getting married in white and damn well entitled to wear it.'*

The following week Bill rang to say his grandmother had invited me to Sunday tea. They lived in a two up, two down terraced cottage, with a small back yard.

With Bill, everything centred around money. If he was skint, we would sit and chat in the kitchen and cook supper together. Sometimes we'd go for a walk or he would come over to our place and bring his jazz records and we'd jive around the room.

One evening he called around the flat, waving an envelope.

'Come on, Monika, put your glad rags on, we're going out tonight. *We're in the money we're in the money,'* he sang, as I looked for something suitable to wear.

He called a taxi and, to my astonishment, it pulled up outside the Grosvenor Hotel.

The menu exceeded my schoolgirl French, I hadn't a clue what to order. I left it to Bill.

'Yes, I'll have the same,' I said, as he spoke in impeccable French to the waiter, I was very impressed.

'This is the life, Monika. When we've got the money we can live it up. If we haven't we can't, it's as simple as that.'

Unfortunately I have never found it quite as simple as that.

Late one afternoon Bill took me into a smart restaurant. We hadn't eaten all day and the smell of food was intoxicating. We sat and looked at the menu. I was famished. As the waiters passed our table carrying plates of delicious food the various aromas gnawed away at my stomach. Bill leaned over to whisper in my ear. Something romantic? Hardly.

'In a minute,' he said, 'I am going to ask you what would you like to eat. For God's sake don't ask for anything, just say a cup of coffee.'

I nodded wearily.

'What would you care to eat, darling?' he said in a loud voice. 'How about the rainbow trout with almonds, or the *Boeuf bourguignon*?'

'I am sorry, darling,' I said, my stomach emitting a high-pitched groan, 'I really couldn't eat another morsel after that huge lunch at the Savoy.' I was keeping my end up. 'I'll just have a very small coffee.'

'Are you sure, dear?'

'Positive,' I said.

'Waiter, two small coffees please.'

Later I had to empty my purse to pay both our fares home. It was great fun while it lasted but money was meaningless to him. Bill held money like a burning ember. When you are young and without a care in the world, the devil-may-care attitude can seem attractive and highly amusing. When Bill became serious and mentioned that *ting* ... marriage, for me it was too risky a proposal.

Today he writes popular television scripts and has entertained and made many people laugh. In the same way as he entertained and made a young nurse laugh ... many years ago.

Chapter Ten

Postmen, meter readers and district nurses have at least one thing in common – *dogs*. Not that we don't like them, it's when we enter their domain, they have strict rules as to whom they will give credence to as friend or foe.

The fact that on your last visit you had to endure a tail-wagging whiplash from some mutt fit to bruise the legs for weeks, or one of Pavlov's dogs drooling all over you from eyelid to toenail, is no guarantee you will receive the same reception two weeks or even two days running.

The size of a canine is a poor indicator of the greeting you will receive. Much has to do with your voice, demeanour, clothes and above all the correct doggy perfume, which can be liver, ouzo or bone.

Another important issue to consider is your affinity with dogs. To enter a house trembling, hyperventilating and cowering in a corner will give off fear vibes of an imminent attack, which in turn triggers a paranoid canine response. If an explanation to the canine is not forthcoming within ten seconds, he is likely to go into an attacking mode.

Waving a white flag will not wash with the canine. This could signal playtime and have him tugging tenaciously throughout your visit.

Unfortunately, Gladiator, Mrs Nash's dog, was having his mid-morning kip when I called. My knock on the porch door disturbed him. He was upset and not a happy chappie. As soon as he heard me, he thrust his huge muscular body with all the force he could muster, which was considerable, at the glass door. Through it I could see the drooling fangs of an Alsatian. He growled. Then mistaking me for a dentist, decided to show me his sharp white molars through the glass. As I was pondering whether the panes were reinforced, Gladiator decided to hurl his athletic torso at the door frame again, the flimsy structure pulsating, as in a hurricane.

I reached in my bag for one of my regular cards:

> *The district nurse called today*
> *and was unable to find you in.*
> *Please ring Rod 6206 to arrange another visit.*

I rested the card on the glass partition to sign my name, but the dog was determined to deter me once and for all. He reversed a few steps in order to gather momentum, then his splayed legs left the ground, letting fly at the door. There was an almighty crack as he thrust with all his might towards me, shattering the glass. I decided not to stay to examine the damage and retreated next door to Janet Simpson, a former patient.

'May I use your telephone?'

'Of course, nurse. Come in.' Janet led me into her kitchen and handed me the telephone.

'Would you happen to have Mrs Nash's number?'

'Yes, she let me have it when she had the flu.'

I dialled the number. I could hear it ringing next door. The kitchens overlooked each other and from the kitchen window, I could see Mrs Nash enter and pick up the receiver.

'Mrs Nash,' I began, 'it's the district nurse.

Do you think you could have your dog tied up when I visit you?'

'Of course, nurse. Mind you, Gladdy wouldn't hurt a fly, he's a real softie.'

'I'm sure he is, Mrs Nash.'

'I will have him tied up before you arrive. Where are you at the moment?'

'Next door,' I said nervously.

She swung around and looked through the kitchen window and started to wave and laugh. Somehow I didn't think she would find the damaged porch so amusing.

Major, a Great Dane, was another gargantuan canine. He was such a mound of a dog that a basket had not yet been invented that would accommodate him. He usually slept on a single divan bed where he could stretch his frame to its fullest extent. Today he had other plans. When I reached the bend of the stairs, there was Major filling the entire space.

'Just step over him,' the son instructed me, 'he's very docile.'

I warily raised one leg over his trunk and was just about to bring the other over when he woke up. On seeing me and with his military background, he decided to stand to attention.

This was no time for Major to think he was on parade, not with me astride like a donkey on Margate sands. I was terrified that we

123

would both fall downstairs. I just managed to grab the banister rail and propel myself, in a crumpled heap, back on to the stairs. As I tried to stand up, my gymnastic demonstration concluded in an ungainly version of the splits. Unlike Marilyn Monroe, fortunately I *was* wearing something underneath my dress; nevertheless it would have still educated Marcus. As he helped me to my feet his face flushed. I was wearing the latest craze in pants, passionate purple.

His mother, Mrs Watt, was an extremely rude individual and not given to polite exchanges or even an elementary please or thank you. I cannot remember seeing her smile in all the time I attended her. The corners of her mouth permanently drooped, having drained to the last dregs the cup of misery. She lay on her sand-coloured sofa like a beached whale with the expectation of an immediate response to her every demand.

She clicked her fingers and grunted her orders.

'Andrews, over here. I need you. Pick that comb up, put it over there. You idiot, over there, I said.'

Miss Andrews, her back bent and wearing a mask of acquiescence, ingratiated herself to perpetual humiliation. Having worked for Mrs Watt since she was fourteen, over the years Miss Andrews had become a caricature of Mrs Watt herself. She took pleasure in taking out *her* frustrations on Doreen, the housemaid.

The house was one of several large properties on the fringe of Forest Hill, near Horniman's Museum. You would think that it had taken the overflow, with its proliferation of ancient artefacts and statues.

The hall was a marble chessboard. In the centre was a large white statue of a Greek god, minus fig leaf. Judging by the son's collection of paintings of Adonis in his downstairs cloakroom and his pen and ink sketches of male torsos, I imagine this statue was his idea.

Miss Andrews, anxious to quell any excitement for anyone passing the sculpture, had obscured his anatomy with a fluffy yellow duster. Naturally this had the reverse effect and became the focus of attention. Having an analytical mind, even I had to reassure myself that he had in fact only lost his fig leaf and that there weren't any other parts of the sculpture missing.

Persian tapestries and oriental paintings hung from the walls. Unlike the museum, where each room carried a theme, the house was a hotchpotch of different countries.

Doreen was making tea in the kitchen when she beckoned me in.

'I'm leaving next month to get married,' said the maid. 'Gawd knows how I've lasted so long in this place. Miss Andrews is always picking on me. She only sticks it herself 'cos she thinks the old bag is going to leave her something when she pops her clogs. Mrs Watt promised Miss Andrews that if she stayed, she would make sure that she was comfortable in her old age. Huh, some hopes. That probably means she'll leave her one cushion. You wouldn't believe how mean she is. Take Christmas, she always makes such a fuss at giving us all a present. I've been here five years and each year all she has ever given me was *one* embroidered handkerchief. Not even a box of three. My Derek reckons she'll probably give us *one* teaspoon, for a wedding present.'

As I left it started to rain. Marcus stopped me on my way out. He was what his mother called *something in the city*. Whatever that certain something was, he looked the part. At the time there seemed to be a lot of men that passed through the portals of railway and underground stations heading for destinations unknown. Doubtless the same individuals who as teenagers at public school despised wearing school uniform and couldn't wait to toss it aside and, for many, their good manners with it, had now adopted the *something in the City* uniform: the bowler hat, the rolled umbrella, a copy of *The Times* under one arm, a briefcase complete with sandwiches hidden under important-looking documents. Those who carried documents stamped *Highly Confidential* or *Top Secret*, having probably stamped them themselves, felt obliged to bring them out of the briefcase during the journey for an airing to add an air of importance and mystery to their otherwise tedious or mundane job as a civil servant.

Quite why some of these pompous, arrogant individuals carried the title *civil* when civility was alien to them, was beyond me. They had this supercilious look stamped on their faces to indicate that all other travellers were invisible. Especially the heavily pregnant lady with the tired, anxious expression. Or the elderly, strap-hanging gentleman struggling to remain upright. Incidentally, whatever happened to all those bowler hats?

The *sardine tin* method of travelling was not for Marcus. Marcus had a Roller.

'Do you have your own transport, nurse?'

My chance of a ride in a Rolls-Royce was limited to my admission to the celestial choir with my toes turned up. I was not about to forfeit the opportunity.

Pride prevented me from mentioning my normal mode of transport and I found myself lying, 'I'm on foot actually.'

I sank into the sumptuous seating, sliding my palms over the soft interior. This was sheer luxury. The comfort, the smell of leather. I took a deep breath and briefly closed my eyes. Marcus was my chauffeur, and I was the duchess. I savoured the illusion for all of five minutes.

'I would like to get off at the Cherry Tree public house, please,' I said in my best elocutionary trained voice, courtesy of the school assembly. A session that we were subjected to, sandwiched between deportment and how to blow one's nose correctly in public. These three subjects have proved of utmost importance in my career, as you can imagine. Invaluable when one finds oneself working in these salubrious upper crust areas, but not a lot of use, I admit, for my regular clientele in Brixton or Camberwell.

The pub at East Dulwich was near to a bus stop. Fifteen minutes later I arrived back at the house to pick up my bike, which I had propped on the outside wall.

The front door opened and for a second time the son stepped out, this time carrying his briefcase, which he had obviously forgotten.

I vaulted onto the bike and pedalled furiously. The thought of trying to think of a logical explanation made me pedal all the faster.

Topsy was a little white poodle that I was very fond of. His owner was suffering from tuberculosis and I visited to give her streptomycin injections. Streptomycin was discovered in the 1940s and was one of the first effective treatments for the disease. It is still used today for resistant strains.

I would usually visit late morning and the patient would still be resting in bed. Our instructions were that TB patients must not be visited when the district nurse could be tired and susceptible to contracting the disease herself.

On my arrival, the dog would be hiding under the bedspread. No duvets then. I'd call her name and watch her move. She would burrow the length and breadth of the bed, in an effort to find an exit to greet me.

'Where's Topsy?' I asked one morning, when I couldn't see her burrowing under the bedclothes.

'She's ashamed of herself,' said the husband, 'she's hiding in the wardrobe.' He opened the wardrobe door and pulled back the row of clothes to reveal one shivering, shorn poodle. She had been clipped in the traditional way and was disgusted with her appearance. It would take a couple of weeks for the dog to start socialising again.

Henry was a brown and white terrier.

'Henry will be all right as long as you don't bend down. As soon as you bend down he will go for you,' said the owner of an innocent, eager-looking puppy.

Wonderful, so how do I bed-bath this lady

without bending down?

I opened the airing cupboard and took out the towels ... Henry watched. When I went into the kitchen to boil the water, he followed me. The watchful eye accompanied me back into the bedroom. It followed my every movement.

I brought the large enamel bowl to the bedside and, bending my knees, I slowly lowered my body, still holding the heavy bowl, and carefully placed it on the table. So far so good, but Henry was eyeing me suspiciously, just waiting for an opportunity. I did the same manoeuvre when placing the towels in position. As soon as I bent over the bed to remove the patient's nightdress, Henry gave a warning growl. I dropped slowly to my knees. The whole procedure had me grovelling on my knees, moving up and down the sides of the bed on all fours like a toddler. At least I had managed it without incurring the wrath of this bad-tempered terrier. I was glad to stand up after the bed bath was over, to stretch my legs.

Instinctively, I leaned over the patient to straighten her pillows to make her comfortable before I left. I could hear the sound of distant rumbling like thunder, then a louder growl – then the leap.

Henry was on my back, hanging on by his teeth to my new cardigan. I quickly unbuttoned it and successfully shook him off, only for him to make another flying leap.

Without thinking, I bent down to pick up the cardigan from the floor. Before I could say Bob Martin, he had managed to latch his jaws onto a sizeable amount of material that comprised of the rear end of my knickers, together with a chunky portion of flesh.

I decided to swipe him a blow with the towel, but still he clung on tenaciously. I grabbed a large vase of flowers and drenched him. Reluctantly he let go.

'Henry is naughty, isn't he. You really mustn't bend down as he only wants to play.'

Uniform was another thing that district nurses had in common with postmen and meter readers: we all wore a type of uniform. The style of district nurses' hats had changed, which gave rise to some confusion with the public. I was even stopped in the street and asked if I was on my way to the Girl Guides hall, and could I take her daughter?

The hospital request for Mrs Moat was for a one-off visit. She was having a bowel X-ray and needed to have an enema the day before. She seemed flustered when I called.

'Oh it's you,' she said.

'Where do you want me to go?' I asked.

'The usual place, of course,' she said.

'Where's that?' I asked.

She pointed to a door in the hall.

'OK,' I said, and opened the door expecting her to follow me.

I could see that the area was extremely small. It was little more than a small cupboard.

'I can't do it in there,' I said.

'Why not?' she said indignantly. 'Everyone else does.'

'What! In that small space?'

'No one has complained before, they just take a torch in with them.'

'To do an enema?'

'Oh, I'm sorry, is it the nurse? I thought you'd come to read the meter!'

A couple of weeks later I happened to run into a lady meter reader at a house I was visiting. With amusement, I told her about the incident of mistaken identity.

'That's nothing, I was in Herne Hill last week and as soon as I knocked on the door of the bungalow, the man grabbed my hand and said, *"Quick, in here"* and shoved me in the bedroom. I wondered what was going on. His wife was in bed in labour. Her pains were coming every minute! I don't wear my hat now. Phew, I don't want to go through that again.'

'I suppose if I had to,' I said, 'I could manage to read the meter.'

'I could have done the enema OK.'

'They're not always easy,' I said.

'I don't think it would have been a problem, I've had some experience.'

'Oh, really?'

'I used to be a petrol pump attendant,' she said with a grin.

Shortly after my visit to Mrs Watt, I heard that she had died. The local newspaper published her will. Naturally the bulk of her estate went to her only son, Marcus. Then there was a long list of beneficiaries, mostly animal charities. Major was left £1,000, the equivalent of about £10,000 today. I glanced down the list for Miss Andrews' name.

At the end of the list was mentioned the sum of £100 for her faithful housekeeper Miss Andrews. Forty years of kowtowing on a promise and then the old lady had reneged. After all that time, £100 was an insult.

One thing I did learn about nursing the rich and the poor. You rarely have to search for the relatives of a dying, wealthy person. Many bees buzz around the money pot. Sadly, many poor die alone.

Chapter Eleven

My mother was coming up from Kent and we had arranged to meet at Kings Cross Station. For some time now, her letters had indicated her anxiety about the sort of people I might meet in London. Living in sin city, as she called it. I had left home at sixteen, and my mother seemed to have locked me into those pubescent years and thrown away the key. It was time to show her the mature woman that I thought I was. I invited her to stay a few days to try to dispel some of her fears.

I arrived early and walked over to a newsvendor. His cry as like a singing mantra: *'Staaaar – Neeeews* or *Standard.'* As I listened to him I thought about some of the fast disappearing cries of London. The totter with his horse and cart collecting scrap would call out with the last word sounding like the dying drone of an air raid siren, 'Raaaags, bones and rabbit skiiiins.'

My favourite was the scruffily clad man who sat cross-legged with a greasy cap at his feet, drawing the most wonderful colourful pavement drawings in chalk. They were a joy to see. When passers-by tossed coins in his cap, his reply was always the same: 'Thank you very much, sir/madam – could do with more.'

I strolled into the station café and looked at the front page of The Standard. It was difficult to concentrate as some of the passengers hurried off the train and began to converge on the café.

Some businessmen dawdled for some time, drinking numerous cups of coffee, their ashtrays forming a pyramid of cigarette stubs.

One man looked decidedly agitated and fiddled with his tie and fingered his cuff links. His eyes darted nervously towards the open door. Two other smartly dressed businessmen in their late fifties were engrossed in conversation at the next table.

'Wait until you see mine, Baz. She's a lovely young thing and when she's dressed up as a school girl in her gymslip, she's a smasher.'

Two young girls in their twenties, both in tight split skirts, wiggled their way into the café arm in arm and walked straight up to their table.

'Hallo Stanley, how lovely to see you,' said the blonde, in a simpering, syrupy voice. Stanley stood up. She kissed him on the lips.

'Hallo darling, you're looking lovely.'

She then introduced her skinny dark-haired friend to Basil. They shook hands which, given the situation, looked somewhat incongruous. The men stood up and linked arms with the girls. Both were young enough to be their daughters. The blonde girl spoke again.

'We're going to give you a good time,' she said, with a plastic smile.

Judging by her tangerine face pack with two cherry blobs for cheeks and skimpy outfit, she looked remarkably like the good time that was said to have been had by all. This was *not* the sort of scene for my mother to see, so I decided to wait outside the café on the platform.

'Hallo missy, can you spare a copper for a bowl of soup?'

I spun round to see a 'gentleman of the road' whose face was very familiar to me. It was Reilly, whom I had first met in Casualty and then when he was a patient on the TB ward. The hospital ward is a great leveller. Once a man is bathed, hair cut, shaved and in hospital pyjamas, on looks alone there is little to distinguish him from the man in the next bed. Reilly *could* have chosen to melt into the background. No, not him. Reilly was not a happy individual, he was a moaner.

'This food's like pig swill,' he'd say.

'Well, you must have tasted it to know,' said one patient.

'I'm used to better food that this. Who's

put bricks in this bed? I'm used to my comfort. Nurse, this sheet's scratchy, there's too much starch in it.'

Now here he was with his begging bowl. I once read that each year for a week a priest dressed up as a tramp and lived with them so that he could understand true poverty. Whenever I met a tramp, I could never be quite sure whether it was the priest or a true vagrant. I knew Reilly wasn't a priest, but I was a soft touch. As I opened my purse I could see my mother waving and hurrying towards me. I snatched a couple of coins, unaware of their value until I placed them in his hand. I had given him five shillings – enough for five bowls of soup. He kissed the coins and gave me a wet kiss on the lips. At that moment my mother stood beside me; her face, etched in disgust, said it all.

'God luv yer, me darlin',' he continued. 'You're an angel, a bloody angel.'

We walked out of the station to the sound of Reilly calling after us, 'I'll not forget you, missy. I'll look out for you again.' I felt quite sure he would too.

I told my mother how Reilly had been the bane of my life. The first time we met was in Casualty. A few days before Christmas, or during a particularly harsh winter, a lot of tramps would *conveniently* collapse outside the hospital. According to the medical staff, Reilly was a regular.

As the porters wheeled him into Casualty, he looked as though he was gasping his last. The casualty officer spotted him and started shouting, 'It's Reilly, get him out of here.'

'We can't put him out like this,' I said.

'Like what?' he replied.

'Like he's got no pulse,' I said.

That was different. He started barking his orders: 'Quick, oxygen. Heart stimulant – nikethamide? Someone give him mouth to mouth resuscitation. Come on, quickly.'

No one moved.

'Come on someone. Who's going to give him the kiss of life? Nurse?'

'Me?' I said. 'I'm hopeless at it.'

As I mentioned before, it had always been the kiss of death, when I gave it. As soon as I had puckered up my lips and tried to breathe life into someone in cardiac arrest, it was all over and time for the muffled drum.

Having drawn the short straw, Reilly and I became acquainted. This time my technique was different, it was much quicker. His iron constitution, breath reeking of methylated spirits and regurgitated cheese and gherkin sandwich, provided the fuel needed to ignite his engine.

Apprehensively I waited for the results of his sputum test. It proved positive for tubercle bacillus. Now I was fearful as to whether he had given me the kiss of death.

Several blood-sucking sessions later, I was finally given the all-clear from TB at the Path. Lab. I didn't get the all-clear from my mother, after telling her this incident.

'I couldn't believe my eyes when I saw you let that dirty old tramp kiss you,' she said. 'And now you tell me he has TB.'

We did the usual touristy bits, including Trafalgar Square where my mother bought some bird seed to attract the pigeons to perch on the top of my head and crap for the photographer.

For a change I thought we would try an unusual type of restaurant and we made our way to one called the Macabre. The tables were in the shapes of coffins, skulls were placed on them for ash trays and surrounding us on the walls were hand-painted replicas of amusing epitaphs on headstones.

'It's been very nice. I've enjoyed the afternoon and you didn't embarrass me as much as you did your father when he was in London.'

My father had travelled to London to take me home, following my operation to have my appendix removed. He had had a very Victorian upbringing and tried to impose some of what Margaret Thatcher would have called Victorian values on me. He despaired that I would ever become the refined lady he had hoped for in a daughter.

He could easily get embarrassed. On the day of my discharge from hospital, I had a friend bring my clothes to the ward. Unfortunately she had forgotten to pack anything to keep my stockings up. Undeterred, I asked the ward staff for two lengths of bandage to tie around the tops of the stockings.

Dad and I were walking together along the long hospital corridor when I felt something moving give way. It was the bandages. Together with my stockings, they were flapping at my ankles. There was nothing for it, I had to take the stockings off and put them in my pocket. When I looked up, I was on my own. My father had disappeared. I found him later waiting outside the hospital gates.

We got a taxi to the station. In an effort to appear sophisticated I had brought my rainbow-coloured umbrella, of which I was very proud. It was very pretty, multicoloured in a subtle way, ranging from a pale peach to orange then lavender to purple.

I sat in the corner seat of the carriage and made sure that I held it facing the other passengers for them to admire. My father sat in the opposite corner.

The train drew in at Chatham station. A man called to his two children and leaned over me to take two suitcases from the overhead rack. He was holding on to his heavy cases and trying to take charge of two small children at the same time as he made his way to the exit door beside me.

Suddenly I felt something tug at my umbrella. No way would I let go of the handle. I clung on so tightly that I was lifted off my seat and dragged on to the platform. Once on the platform, I discovered the reason. The handle had hooked itself on to the man's braces. I tried hard to hold on to my umbrella, while he tried even harder to hold on to his trousers. Finally I managed to untangle the handle from his braces and jump back on the train.

The compartment was in an uproar. Most of the passengers had witnessed the fiasco.

'How that man didn't lose his trousers, I'll never know.'

'And his reputation,' said another.

'It's not every day we are treated to a Whitehall farce.'

We were all laughing and joking. The ribbing went on for quite a while.

I looked around for my father. He had gone. He did not reappear until we arrived at our destination, then he emerged ... from a separate compartment.

Chapter Twelve

'I think that's marvellous,' I said, 'to reach one hundred and three.'

Dolly, Mrs Hill's daughter, had been showing me the birthday cards and flowers that had started to arrive.

'The Mayor will be coming, Mum, for the tea party,' said Dolly.

'Marvellous, *marvellous?* I think it's disgusting. I should have snuffed it long ago. Look at Dolly, eighty-three and still struggling to look after me.'

'It's all right Mum, with nurse's help I'm coping.'

'Coping, I should have clogged my pops by now ... you know what I mean.'

'Don't take any notice of her, nurse, she's excited really.'

Mrs Hill epitomised everyone's idea of a sweet little old lady. A diminutive woman weighing little more than six stone, she had on an old-fashioned mob-cap framing her pink heavily wrinkled face. Peeping out of the cap were small silver curls, under which was an alert, shrewd mind. Tucked under the wrist band of her pink bed jacket was a lavender-soaked handkerchief. She released it with two fingers and, like a priest with incense, she gently shook it around the bed. The heady aroma wafted across the room.

'What have I got to get excited about? All this fuss because the Mayor is coming with his lavatory chain wrapped round his neck? Much ado about nothing, if you ask me. I've outlived all my friends, what is there left for me to do? The curate from St John's came round the other day and was saying The Lord's Prayer. He got to *Lead me not into temptation.* "Stop!" I said. "Temptation, what sort of temptation have you got in mind? What am I supposed to get into at my age? It's a bit late for me now." Do you know what he said? *You should have thought of a few temptations then, when you had the chance.'*

I gave Mrs Hill her bed bath. The daughter walked with me to the front door.

'Your mother is really funny, the things she comes out with. She is a real sweetie.'

'Do you think so? Do you know, nurse, there are times when she goes on and on about wanting to die that I start thinking I'd like to do her a favour. I don't suppose I would, but she winds me up so. I've had her all my married life. Fred and I had only been married six months when my dad died and Mum arrived on the doorstep *for a few weeks.* She never went back. She ruined our marriage. She always interfered. We had no privacy, no life together. I'll show you something, shall I? She has an old school bell under her bed that she rings all the time for attention. As soon as I let you out of the house, you'll see, she'll start. Call out good-bye and I'll go as if to shut the door. Then you'll see what she's *really* like.'

'Goodbye, Mrs Hill,' I called out, 'I'm going now.'

'Bye bye, nurse,' the old lady replied softly.

The daughter opened and closed the door. There was a sudden screech.

'Dolly, DOLLY, where are you? I want my pillow moved.'

With that she picked up the bell. It clanged and resonated throughout the house. I nodded my head. I was disillusioned. This sweet little old lady was a tyrant. What a hellish life Dolly had with her. All those years of frustration, tension and anger for Dolly and her husband. Their married life had been a sham. Dolly's husband had been dead some twenty years. He must have been a saint. The daughter was a slave to parental loyalty, and in return the mother had embroiled them with emotional blackmail.

One thing I puzzled over, why did she have to give her that huge bell in the first place?

I had arranged to meet Sarah outside Mrs Thorne's house in Dulwich village. The patient had extensive burns to the face and body, but we had no information as to how

144

this had happened. I arrived early to do a recce. and stared in amazement at the massive mansion overlooking Dulwich Park.

District nurses are used to going in a wide range of houses, flats and rooms and become adaptable to any given situation. After a while the nurse will just home in on the patient, the trappings of wealth being superfluous. But there is wealth and there is wow! what am I walking into? Mrs Thorne would fit into the latter.

The family had arranged to meet us there. I waited a short distance from the house so that Sarah and I could go in together.

As I waited, a black limousine glided up to the house. A pin-striped-suited young man, early thirties, emerged, accompanied by a elegant younger blonde woman. She looked every inch the model who had just stepped out of *Vogue*. The only thing missing was an Afghan hound or a Borzoi. This family were not just well off, they were extremely wealthy.

I was glad when I saw Sarah in the distance for moral support. Why had the family not acquired the services of a private nurse? Private nurses from the British Nursing Association were often sought to care for the sick and elderly in an affluent area.

On Christmas Day and other bank holidays, the employer would generously give the private nurse time off. Then to the annoyance of the district nurses, they would be expected to replace the private nurse over the holiday period. We were often treated as skivvies by the PPs (private patients). Was this one?

I am sure we must have let out a small gasp as we followed the relatives into the house; it would have been difficult not to. We stared in stunned silence while the plum embossed carpets gently brushed around our ankles. Large Dutch paintings gazed down at us with their golden frames shimmering as the shafts of sunlight streamed through stained glass windows and danced with the mirrors in the hall. Although our training had instilled in us to appear unimpressed however extravagantly furnished a home might be, it was difficult to maintain a blank expression.

It was like entering a stately home. We could not help our eyes darting in all directions, soaking up the splendour of the opulence.

The son beckoned us to meet the mother. As soon as he spoke, Sarah and I went into shock.

"Ere yer are, Mum. The nurses are 'ere for yer.'

The voice, the accent, were out of place. They did not fit in with this extravagant lifestyle.

Mrs Thorne sat on a plum velvet armchair, with her back to us, smoking. The long kinked ash about to miss the onyx ashtray.

Her nails were polished and manicured. She had two fingers of a 'brown glove', the tell-tale sign of a three-pack-a-day smoker. On her other hand was a padded crepe bandage. Twirled in a careless fashion around her head was a pink silk scarf, which failed in its effort to tame spiked, orange hair.

She turned to look at us. The right side of her face was badly burned and blistered.

'Who the bloody 'ell arst you to come 'ere?' she rasped sharply. 'I never sent for yer.'

'No, Mother, Dr Sharpe did,' said her daughter.

'What yer 'ere for? There ain't nuffink wrong wiv me.'

I felt uneasy. The accent, the opulence, the air of neglect – who were these people? How had they come to be in a place like this? They were obviously from working class backgrounds. Although I wasn't too sure about the daughter, Sally. Why hadn't she got the same cockney accent?

Sarah was chewing all this over in her head too, with her eyebrows raised and her foot increasing its pressure on top of mine.

'We are here to help to dress–' said Sarah.

'Dress, DRESS. I don't need no one to dress me. I can dress meself.'

'Mum,' said her son Tommy, 'the nurses 'ave come 'ere to see to yer burns.'

'I can do 'em meself.' She stroked her

bandaged hand as she spoke.

'You cannot do it, Mother. Come on now, the nurses only want to help you,' Sally said. The daughter stood up. 'Come on, Mother. I'll help you to your bedroom.'

'No,' she said sharply. 'Not in *my* bedroom. No one's going in *my* bedroom. We'll go in the pink guest room.'

The door opened to display a four-poster bed with side steps. Sally showed us into the spacious en-suite bathroom-cum-dressing room. This in itself was a novelty. It was the size of a surgeon's scrub-up room. We laid out our equipment on the long green marble slab.

'The mirrors in the dressing room make it look even bigger,' I whispered to Sarah. 'If this bathroom is only for the guest room, what must hers be like?'

'What have we walked into, Mik?' said Sarah in a low voice.

I shook my head. 'I don't know, there's something weird going on here.'

We used the bathroom as a clinical area to prepare the dressings. As we undressed the patient we noticed a large raw area down the right side of her trunk and leg.

'How did this happen?' I asked.

''ow do I know?' came the reply. I looked across at the daughter. She gave a brief shake of the head and a knowing wink, so that we knew not to discuss the matter any further.

After we had dressed the area, we helped Mrs Thorne downstairs and into her chair. We were then shown into the morning room, where there was a tray of tea and biscuits.

'Sit down,' said Sally. 'I'll be straight. Mother's an alcoholic. She burnt herself smoking in bed. She was so drunk that the bed caught alight and it was some time before she realised. The fact that she had soaked the bed helped to prevent the fire from spreading.'

We came away still completely baffled by the whole situation.

'Do you think they've won the football pools?' Sarah asked.

'I reckon they could be gangsters,' I said, joking.

'Did you notice how the daughter was locking the wardrobes and drawers while we were in the room, Mik?'

'Yes, I thought that was odd. Did she think that we would take something?' I said.

It would be many weeks before the family saga unfolded. Gradually Mrs Thorne started to communicate with us.

'My old man Jimmy, like me, was born in the East End. 'e was from a big family, the youngest of eleven kids. 'is mother 'ad 'im late, see, at forty-five. By the time 'e was going to school, apart from his sister Ruby, she would 'ave been nineteen, the rest of the kids had left 'ome and got families of their own. It was 'is teacher what tried to get 'im on. Mr Marks gave extra lessons in the evenings and Jimmy used to run errands. Mr Marks 'elped 'im get a scholarship for the grammar school and that's 'ow 'e got where 'e did.'

'How is it, Sarah, I got my eleven plus, but I didn't finish up dwelling in marble halls.'

''alls, girl. Don't forget it's 'alls,' laughed Sarah.

'It's certainly a mystery. I reckon it's ill-gotten gains. I think our Mrs Thorne is a gangster's moll,' I said with a laugh.

'Those burns will take months to heal so we have plenty of time for the next instalment. It will probably all surface in the end.'

'What you mean, Mik? When we go there and find the place cleaned out and the police taking fingerprints?'

We didn't have to wait long before Mrs Thorne told us a bit more of her story.

It would seem that at the grammar school the coaching and encouragement continued. The headmaster hoped that Jimmy would stay on at school, but money was short at home and he was forced to leave school at fourteen, though not before the head had got him a job.

When Jimmy left school he had a job as a

junior assistant with a diamond merchant at Hatton Garden. Jimmy was fascinated with all that he saw around him. Although he was employed as an odd job boy at first, sweeping up, taking the post, making endless cups of tea and so on, he never missed an opportunity to ask questions. His boss suggested that if he went to night school, he would consider him for an apprenticeship.

In his last year as an apprentice, he met Mary, Mrs Thorne, a girl he had known from junior school. With his apprenticeship behind him and the prospects of a better wage, they decided to get married. Like many young people at that time they started married life living with his parents in one room.

As things improved, they were able to rent two rooms of their own and start a family. His mother-in-law worked as a cleaner at the town hall and asked her boss if he could put in a good word for them at the housing department. Soon after the second boy was born they were allocated a council flat in South Hackney.

It took months for Mrs Thorne to tell us her life story. We were fascinated. By now, I was visiting her on my own. When I got home, I would try to piece the story together.

'One day, nurse, 'e told me, *now that I'm getting a little more money, what say you if I puts a bit by each week for a deposit to buy our own 'ouse. it won't be anything grand, gal, but it will be our own.*

'"You're bloody bonkers," I told 'im. "People like us can't buy 'ouses," I says.

'"*Why not?*" he says.

'"Cos it ain't done, that's what. That's only for them what's rich. Ain't no one ever 'ad their own 'ouse in our family," I told 'im.

'"*That don't mean we can't be the first, does it?*" Jimmy said.

'"Nah, you're barmy. That's what comes of working wiv all them toffs, it's given you crazy ideas. It's all right for them moneyed people," I says. 'e did save up, and now and again 'e'd say, *Won't be long now, another couple of years,* or, *This time next year we can start looking.* I thought 'e was kiddin'. Then just before Christmas 'e must 'ave been savin' five years, 'e says, *Gal, after Christmas we can start looking now.*

'I know 'e was cleverer than me, so 'e never talked much about 'ow 'e was getting on in the job. 'e used to talk to my dad sometimes. My dad used to say, *Your bloke's going up the ladder like a monkey on a stick.*

'This night Jimmy grabbed me round the waist and lifted me up 'igh in the air, then spun me round. "Put me down, yer fool," I says, "we aint got it yet."'

'*Get your blue dress, Mary, the one with the white collar. We're going out on the town, gal.*

I've asked Mum to give eye to the kids, we're going down the pub for a drink to celebrate and 'ave a bit of a knees-up.

'I couldn't believe it, nurse, we was just ordinary folks. I put me best dress on.'

'Were you excited?' I asked Mrs Thorne.

'Excited, I was as 'appy as a flea in a pet shop. We 'ad everyone buying us drinks and patting Jimmy on the back and pulling 'is leg. *We'll 'ave to pay arf a crown to speak to you two soon,* says one. *'ow d'yer manage that, mate? Been flogging some of the glitter orf the floor?*

'We was a bit tiddly time we got 'ome and 'is mother gave us some dirty looks. We didn't care. She could get jealous. She used to say it wasn't fair that 'er 'usband 'ad worked 'ard all 'is life and 'ad nuffink to show for it. *You youngsters is gonner 'ave everything dropped in yer lap.* I was too 'appy to bover about what she thought. Jimmy reckoned with 'is Christmas bonus I could afford some new curtains and lino. Possibly some bits of second-hand furniture.

'I couldn't wait. The next day I was down the market looking at the curtains. Then, Christmas Eve, Jimmy came 'ome very late. The kids was in bed. 'e looked at me funny like. 'e smelt of whisky – now that was strange for a start, 'e was a bloke for 'is beer.

'*Sit down, Mary. I don't know 'ow you are going to take this,* says Jimmy. *The Guvnor had me in his office this evening. He asked me if I would like to buy in a partnership with 'im.*

'"What does it mean?" I asked. "I don't understand, what are you trying to say?"

'I've got an opportunity, Mary, to buy in a partnership. I could use the money we saved up for the 'ouse, then later on we could probably buy a much better 'ouse, in the country even.

'I remember crying and saying I don't want a bigger 'ouse later, I want a smaller one now.

'Mary, I'll never get the chance again. It means a lot to me, he said. *Later on it could make a lot of difference to both of us. It could turn out to be the best Christmas present we ever 'ad.*

'That night, nurse, I cried myself to sleep. In the morning I gave in. OK, 'ave yer rotten partnership. It could be ten years before we get the chance to buy an 'ouse again.

'Jimmy didn't say any more about it, but I know secretly 'e was pleased. I kept finking – the whole of five years' savings, on a bloody partnership. Course 'is mother lapped it up, kept on about it, fancy wasting all that money and nuffink to show for it.

'I got a little job doing a bit of ironing for a lady. After a few weeks, I bought some new curtains for the flat and a bottle of sherry to cheer me up.

'From then on everything changed. 'e was going to all these meetings. Not just

154

England there was Paris, Amsterdam, 'otel after 'otel, living out of suitcases. 'e loved it. I didn't go with 'im cos I 'ad the kids, see. I went with 'im to the cocktail parties, I 'ad to. Look, there's a photo over there of us taken at the Lord Mayor's Ball.'

I looked at the slim, attractive dark-haired young woman in a slinky dress holding on to the arm of a tall cheerful-looking man. He was in his dinner suit, with an Errol Flynn moustache.

'That was on our birthday. Jim was a year older, but we shared the same day. I'd sooner 'ave 'ad our normal birthday. I used to like going down the pie and mash or 'aving a plate of jellied eels. That'd suit me more than being with these hoity-toity stuck-up lot.

'We 'ad to go to this dinner party. It was all right at first, but when the men went off together and left the ladies, I never knew what to talk about. The women used to rabbit on about the different fancy schools they was going to send their kids to. Or they'd talk about the nanny they'd just got. They knew I wasn't one of them, in the end they would walk away and leave me on me own. I couldn't stand it. But I 'ad to stick it out. When the drinks came round I never refused, it gave me something to do.'

I began to feel sorry for her. I could see how she would be out of her depth.

'I s'pose I started to drink a bit 'eavy like,

155

when Jimmy was abroad. Loneliness. I laugh when I fink 'ow fussy I was, what I'd drink. Later on I couldn't care less. Sometimes Jimmy would take me to some special do. I'd get all dressed up go out, come back and the following day I couldn't remember where I'd been or who I'd spoken to. A complete blank.'

'When did you lose your husband?' I asked.

'About ten years ago.'

'What happened to him?'

'I don't know, I don't want to talk about it.' Immediately the barrier went up again.

'She was just beginning to tell me how she started drinking heavily. Then I went and blew it by asking her how her husband died.'

'Perhaps after all those years she too upset to talk about it,' said Sarah. 'Didn't she say she met him at school? They would have been together a long time, kid.'

'We are still no nearer as to where all this money has come from. The two sons are smartly dressed and drive limos and the daughter, she's in and out all the time. She doesn't seem to work, or need to work. I think the old man took off with some of the diamonds. Maybe he's not dead at all, he's abroad with a new identity and has set the family up with Swiss bank accounts.'

'Mik, I bet it is something really simple, like Mrs Thorne won the football pools.'

'You know, Sarah, after all this time, I can see Dr Sharpe cancelling the visits soon. Her burns have almost healed. We may never know the answer.'

Sarah started to giggle. 'Don't tell me that, girl. It like that serial on the radio I listen to week after week. I hurry home this day for the last one. What happen? Mik fuses every-thing with her new hairdiyer.'

'I know, I was sorry about that.' I started to laugh. 'I hadn't wired the plug properly. It could have been worse, you could have been in the middle of machining something for someone and ruined it.'

'Believe me, Mik, it couldn't be worse. I look forward all day for the end of that story and now I will never know what happened.'

The next time I visited Mrs Thorne, the elder son had managed to get a resident housekeeper for her. Rosie spent a lot of time just listening to her and encouraging her to talk over her problems. The family were distraught about their mother. It was obvious that they had been struggling to deal with her alcoholism for a long time.

When she was in hospital, the family decided that they would get rid of all trace of alcohol. Sally said that they had taken away boxes and boxes of empties. They were hidden all over the house in the strangest places. They had made sure that she hadn't any money in the house to buy any drink.

'The trouble was, nurse, she would just pick out a piece of jewellery and sell it, then go straight to the off-licence.'

As I was leaving, I found Sally crying. It was the anniversary of her father's death. She dried her eyes and said suddenly, 'You are probably wondering where all the money has come from, aren't you?'

I didn't reply.

'Daddy had a partnership in a diamond company. His boss treated him like a son. He used to say that Daddy was the son that he never had. When he died he left my father everything. Daddy took both my brothers into the business. I was sent to a private school. Mum couldn't take any of it in. Too much – too soon. She began drinking all the time. She didn't even bother to hide it. My father stopped taking her to functions. If she wasn't being sick in the lavatory, she was falling about, or creating the most terrible scenes. Daddy often had to send her home by taxi.'

'What happened to your father?' I asked her.

'She killed him.'

I began to shiver and my arms sprang goose-pimples.

'God, what do you mean?' I asked.

'She as good as killed him, as if she had a gun in her hand. Daddy had chronic asthma and used an inhaler. The doctor said he had a bad asthma attack. It looked as though he had called out to my mother to hand him the inhaler and his pills. We found my father dead in the chair. She was sprawled across the floor, drunk, with the inhaler in her hand,' said Sally. 'She was even drunk at the funeral and started shouting in the church. I can never forgive her.'

Chapter Thirteen

'Sarah, I'm on tonight for late-night visits.'

'Uh, huh,' mumbled Sarah, who was writing a letter home.

'I have a late-night morphine, Mrs Thompson. I can't go too early, I shall want to settle her for the night.'

'Right,' said Sarah, preoccupied. 'What time will you be back?'

'It's not that, she's at Brixton, Somerleyton Road.'

Sarah sat up with a jolt. 'What! Why didn't you say? You can't go there on your own. That place is bad news, worse for white people. A white girl was knifed in Somerleyton last Saturday. When you go?'

'I've a couple in Camberwell, I'll be coming from Daneville Road, say, nine thirty?'

'OK. I'll meet you outside the Maudsley. If someone hit me over the head before you get there, at least I'm at the right hospital for head injuries,' she joked.

During the day, Somerleyton Road gave a sense of unease. An unnerving stillness, an atmosphere of foreboding. People sat slouched on the stone steps leading up to the tenement houses, smoking and talking, reminiscent of an American film I'd seen, set in the Bronx. Young men loitered aimlessly and congregated in groups. A feeling of apathy and despair pervaded. Hardly a week would pass, without one reading of crime and violence in this district.

We set off along Coldharbour Lane towards Brixton and turned left into Somerleyton Road. At night the area took on a sinister tone. The groups had become gangs. They no longer remained silent: their voices became louder as they gathered momentum. They were more abusive and fights would break out. We were instructed to go out in twos at night.

We cycled half way down the row of overcrowded, dilapidated houses until we reached Pat Thompson's flat. Then we locked our bikes and hurried up the now deserted steps, flanked by solid balustrading, to the front door. Her husband took us into the dimly lit room. Pat was propped up in bed.

'It's very good of you nurses to come out like this to my Pat. I'll fetch you some water.'

Pat was desperately ill with terminal cancer, her eyes were hollow, her face lacked bloom and her skin was tightly drawn, like dusty grey parchment. We crouched down and introduced ourselves to the gaunt West Indian woman. Instinctively, we each took hold of one of her hands to comfort her.

'How are you feeling tonight, Pat?' I asked.

She shook her head. 'Oh nurse, I have plenty pain, I just don't know how I can put up with much more. My husband is good, but we have two kids. It too much for one man to look after me as well.'

Her eyes welled and tears slowly trickled onto her sunken cheeks. Her husband came in carrying a bowl of warm water, and endeavoured to sound cheerful.

'Don't you worry about me, precious, I'm fine. God give me strength every day. He watch over us. Isn't that right, nurse?'

Sarah took a wet face cloth and gently smoothed it over Pat's forehead and wiped away her tears, as I started to draw up the morphine.

'Yes, that's right, Mr Thompson, said Sarah, *'and he shall wipe away all tears, there will be no more pain, he will make all things new.'*

Pat was sweating and in a lot of pain.

'Them words is nice, nurse,' said Pat in a weak voice.

'Yes, thank you for them, nurse. From the good book, yes?' asked the husband.

Sarah nodded. We were both trying to fight back the tears. I gave Pat the injection. We could see that Pat's life was slipping away and I found it difficult to find her pulse, it was so weak and thready. Sarah helped me to wash Pat, change the bed and give her a mouthwash. We gently rested her back on her pillows and made her comfortable.

'Perhaps you will get some sleep now,' said Sarah.

There was a sudden commotion outside, with men's voices shouting and screeching. Mr Thompson moved to the window and peered carefully through a small gap in the curtain, trying not to draw attention to himself.

'It that bad lot again, they always causing bother. It difficult for my Pat to sleep with all that noise, it not as though I can explain and ask them to keep quiet. They only laugh and make worse noise if I do that. Once she have her injection, if she can't sleep it make her feel bad.'

I went back to the bedside and held Pat's hand gently. Her eyes were closing.

'You will sleep tonight, Pat, and we will see you again.'

She opened her eyes, looked at me, gave a faint smile, then shook her head from side to side. I squeezed her hand, she softly pressed mine. I felt a lump in my throat and turned to brush away a tear. I beckoned to Sarah and whispered, 'I can hardly get a pulse.'

Sarah felt her wrist and shook her head. It was hard, as young nurses, no matter how professional, no matter how many times we had seen this before, not to feel moved to tears. We who could live, laugh and love, to watch a girl of similar age, who wanted all those things, but whose young life was ebbing away.

'When you nurses' ready I take you down the steps, in case of trouble.' Mr Thompson looked anxious. I went over and spoke to him quietly.

'I don't think Pat has very long with us. Her pulse is weaker. Please don't worry about us, we can see ourselves out.'

'Oh no, you girls have been good enough to come here. I'll take you down the steps.' Mr Thompson took us by the arm and hurried us down the steps before disappearing inside the house.

A gang of black youths hovered a few yards up the road. They saw us, turned and one shouted, 'Look at that snowball. What she doing with our sister?'

We tried to unlock our bikes. Sarah said in

a loud voice, 'Mik, don't take any notice. They scum.'

My fingers wouldn't move. 'I can't unlock this damn bike now,' I muttered to myself.

'Scum. She say we scum. Shut your beak – who straighten your nigger knots?' bellowed the big man.

I wrenched the lock off. The chain fell to the ground. I panicked and thought that one of them would pick it up.

'Come on, Sarah, for God's sake.'

Sarah faced them defiantly. 'You make me SICK. You supposed to be MY people? If I had a tommy-gun, I'd shoot the lot of you.'

All at once, they ran en masse towards us.

'Sarah... MOVE,' I shrieked.

We leapt on our bikes and pedalled furiously. We didn't dare look back. A stone whizzed by my ear. Another hit my neck. A sharp pain and my neck and back felt wet. Sweat? Blood?

I didn't know. I didn't care. A bottle hit Sarah's back. I heard her cry out, and saw the bottle smash to the ground.

'Keep going, Mik. I've been hit.'

'Don't stop now,' I shouted back.

Stones hit our wheels. My legs were moving, but the wheels were slowing down. Please God, no not a puncture now. We cycled even faster. My legs ached. My legs heavy. They felt encased in cement. At last the end of the road. I could see two men gaining on us. I felt their hot breath on my neck. Then they were laughing. Squealing. Triumphant.

My lungs felt ready to collapse. Another bottle flew our way. We dodged it. Saw it smash against the wall.

'Hey, what about *white stuff?*' called one.

'Yeah, they could have some. Get it,' said the other.

The big man thundered, 'Then waste them, waste them.'

At this, we seemed to get our second wind and propelled ourselves around the corner into Coldharbour Lane. We didn't stop until we reached the end of the road and into Camberwell. Once home, we flung ourselves exhausted on the sofa.

'I can't believe it, Mik. Those men are the worst, they're crims, thugs. They caught your face – have a look in the mirror.' I had a large cut on my cheek and on the back of my neck.

'Your hair is all matted with blood,' I said.

'Just a minute, kid, you mean my nigger knots.' She grinned. 'I haven't heard that saying since I left Jamaica.' She looked in the mirror. 'It's not too bad kid it could have been a lot worse.'

'Worse? That was bad enough for me. Imagine having to live in that area.'

'I can't see Pat making it through the night, can you?' said Sarah.

'No, I don't think so. I could hardly feel her pulse. It's very sad.'

Before we left in the morning, we heard through the office that Pat had died thirty minutes after we left.

I had to cycle to Brixton that day. I glanced up at Somerleyton Road. A few men sat on some steps, talking. Looking furtively from side to side. I continued on my way and turned left into Railton Road.

Fear and tension smouldered in these streets. It just needed a spark to ignite the touch paper. Time was running out. A few years later the area would become a battle-field, the scene of the Brixton Riots.

Chapter Fourteen

Sylvia lived in Herne Hill in a tree-lined avenue. Her house lay back from the road in a hollow with a gentle slope leading to the front door. Here you could find retired teachers and working professionals, living in small houses with leaded windows and colourful stained glass fanlights. Most had neat gardens to the front and rear.

In Sylvia's garden was an apple tree. Its snowy blossom had fallen and veiled the tidy lawns and shrubs. It was like entering a different county and hard to believe I was still in London. It reminded me of Kent with its apple and cherry blossom and the great variety of orchards that gave popularity to coach trips called blossom drives and to the county's recognition as the garden of England.

Sylvia Field had never objected to children laughing and playing in her garden. I rather suspect she encouraged it. At ninety, she harvested her pleasures where she could. Later, when the tree was bent with the weight of the fruit, two boys from the neighbourhood could be seen picking up 'the drops'.

For some time, Sylvia had been finding it difficult to tend to the lawns and shrubs. Her neighbour Alex came up with a suggestion. If he took on a part of her garden for a vegetable patch, in return he would keep the rest of the garden tidy.

Alex's wife kept an eye on the old lady and chatted to her when she saw her sitting on her rustic seat. She also made sure that whenever she was making a midday meal she would plate one up and hand it over the fence to Sylvia.

'I was sorry to hear about you losing your dog,' Alex said to Sylvia one day. 'I shall miss seeing her about. I expect she was good company for you.'

Sylvia put her handkerchief to her red-rimmed eyes.

'Yes,' she nodded, 'Tammy was a good pal to me.'

Tammy had kept Sylvia on the move. On cold wet mornings when she would have rather have hugged the sheets, she knew that she had to get up and take the dog for its walk. Some of the residents had retired, and if they spotted Sylvia with her dog they would stop for a natter.

After Tammy died, Alex noticed Sylvia seemed vague. Her sprightly walk had slowed to a hobble. Alex's wife Betty was also worried, she had noticed that she had started to talk about her husband as though he were still alive. He had been dead for forty years.

'I must go now, Betty,' she had said. 'Arthur will be home from work shortly and I must get his meal ready.'

'Alex,' said Betty, 'do you think I should get the doctor out to her?'

'You can't very well, love. Not without her permission.'

'I thought the doctor might notice she was acting a bit strange.'

'Betty, at ninety, he'd say, *What do you expect?*'

'Mm, you're right. Have you ever been inside the house, Alex?'

'Nope, never needed to. The lawn mower and all the tools I need are in the shed.'

'Kitty, opposite, said that Sylvia used to

have the paraffin man call. Apparently he's stopped delivering now.'

'Perhaps she got electric fires now,' said Alex. 'I don't know, you women always want to know what's going on in someone else's house.'

'It's not that, I'm not trying to be nosy. I just wondered if she was OK, that's all.'

'Yeah, she's fine, that old lady. Tough as Kelly's boots.'

The following morning, Alex awoke to hear gravel being thrown at the window. He looked at the clock. 'Damn, so much for a lie in on a Sunday.'

'What the hell's going on?' said Betty. 'It's only eight o'clock.'

He looked out of the window to see two small boys waving their arms. He lifted the sash window up and leaned out of the window to call to them.

'If it's a ball in my garden, you can just wait until I get up.'

'No, mister, it's Mrs Field. Something's happened to her.'

Alex pulled his trousers over his pyjamas and took his jacket from the chair.

'You'd better get up, Betty. I might need your help.'

The children took Alex to the old bench in the garden, where they had found Sylvia dressed only in a nightdress and purple with cold. At first they thought she was dead.

The ambulance men found she was unconscious. After the ambulance had gone, Betty and Alex went back indoors. Betty sat at the kitchen table, her head in her hands.

'I can't believe what we have just seen in there, Alex.'

'They'll have to get the Public Health in and sort it all out.'

'I feel sick,' said Betty. 'Not just what we've seen, but to think we lived next door and saw her every day and allowed it to happen.'

'You can't blame yourself, Betty. From all outward appearances, if you judged her garden you would expect the inside to look as neat. The ambulance men said it was hypothermia. They're not sure whether she'll pull through, love. She could have been there all night, and the temperature plummeted last night. It was cold for the time of year.'

'She certainly can't come home to that mess in there if she does recover. I think we should go and see the welfare woman. I know she's supposed to check on the elderly as well as babies.'

I heard what had happened to Mrs Field through the surgery. I met the neighbours there, when they called in with their concerns. Then Jean, the health visitor, asked me to meet Sylvia on the ward. Jean was anxious as the consultant was insistent on discharging Mrs Field home, regardless of the circumstances of her admission.

'According to the neighbours, her home is not safe. The paraffin man refused to leave any more paraffin when he saw water dripping from the electric sockets. He thought the house only needed a spark and it could go up like a tinder box,' I said.

'I've heard that the ward sister and the consultant are going out together,' said the health visitor. 'If so, she could have some influence over the consultant's decision. He may listen to her. Shall we see if she will go with us?'

'That's a good idea,' I said. 'If it's as bad as they say, she may be able to talk him round.'

The ward sister was delighted that we had asked her to go to Sylvia Field's house.

'How splendid, I've never been out in the community before. I've always wanted to see what it was like,' she said excitedly.

'She could be in for a shock,' I whispered to Jean. 'The neighbours reckon they heard some scratching noises, so there could be some "rodies" in there.'

'Oooh, that may not go down very well,' said Jean.

'I won't be a minute,' said Sister O'Neil. 'I'll just make a list. Mrs Field's been asking for some items to be collected from her home.'

On paper, Mrs Field lived in a select area

and the garden back and front gave every appearance of a smart house. Once inside, it was apparent that it was a shack. I found my feet sinking in the papier mâché floorboards. There were dog turds everywhere with their furry growth of fungus. The air was cold and dank and a sour, rancid smell lingered throughout.

I trod warily through to the main living area. Three-foot-high conical mounds of what once resembled clothes were stacked like chairs in a mission hall. One pile consisted of underwear and night clothes, another woollen skirts and jumpers.

We gazed in silence. To our astonishment, Sister O'Neil took out her 'shopping list'.

'Ah,' she said, 'Mrs Field wanted some night attire. I might find something here.' She made her way to one of the bundles of clothes. Jean and I made a grab for Sister O'Neil and pulled her away from the heaps of mouldy clothes.

'What do you think you are doing?' said Jean. 'There could be mice nesting in there.'

'Surely not. Don't be silly, Mrs Field is such a clean little lady,' said Sister.

Jean and I exchanged knowing glances. Sister O'Neil had a lot to learn about the community.

We looked at what was ironically called the toilet. It was nothing more than a toilet seat on top of a bucket. Huge holes in the floorboards made it dangerous for more than one person to go in and inspect it at any one time.

We wandered into the bedroom and living room, not fully able to comprehend how the house had got into such a dilapidated state, without any intervention. Bare electrical wires were hanging from the walls, stripped of their protective coat and dripping in water that was cascading through the ceiling. Water was leaking out of the wall plugs and through an electric light bulb. Little wonder that the man from the hardware store no longer considered it safe to leave paraffin for her.

We thought we had seen enough to convince the consultant that this was not the ideal place to send an elderly lady home to. Especially one that had nearly died of hypothermia.

We walked into the kitchen. Under a heavy layer of soot, we could see that the table had been prepared for a meal. Plates, cutlery, bowls and cups were all covered in a thick black dust. Cobwebs stretched from cup to cup. We stood in stunned silence as though looking at a film set of *Great Expectations*.

There was a sudden movement, a scratching, tapping sound coming from behind the boiler. I looked again at the black substance scattered all over the table. It was not soot or dust.

'Keep still,' I said. 'There are rats in here. The black stuff – it's rat droppings.'

'Don't be ridiculous,' exclaimed Sister O'Neil, 'it can't be.'

Jean took another look. 'She's right.'

'Oh God, how ghastly, how horrible, how can people *live* like this.'

On the word *live*, she did the unforgivable – with her fist clenched she thumped it down on the table like a gavel at an auction, rattling the plates and sending out an alarm signal. Instantly the source of the sound appeared from behind the boiler.

Rats ... scuttled and darted in our direction.

Jean was off and could have beaten today's Linford Christie to the front door. An hysterical Sister O'Neil made a rapid second exit. Once again I found I had my concrete boots on. Unable to move a muscle, I shut my eyes tight. The tension caused the feeling of red hot wires piercing my eyes. I waited for the inevitable.

The needle-like claws of the rodent army trampled over my feet in hot pursuit. I felt a pain in my stomach. My mouth opened to scream, no sound emerged. I was mute... My heart pounded... Then silence. My body shook violently. Then stopped. Perspiration seemed to drain from every pore. My legs felt useless, but I had got to get out of the house. Slowly I made my way to an exit. I had been gripped by terror and anger. When I got outside the house I screamed at O'Neil, 'You damn fool, don't you dare do that again.'

On the way back in Jean's car, Sister O'Neil tried to apologise. I brushed it aside.

'Forget it, all I want from you is to take everything that you have seen today back to your consultant – the shock, the smell, the whole sickening scene.'

A smart tree-lined district, but who can judge with certainty what lies behind the lace curtains?

Many white people would repeatedly speak of the homes of black people being dirty. I don't know how many homes I must have entered. Really entered, not just stood on the doorstep. Walked in the bedroom, the kitchen, the sitting room. The dirtiest homes that I have ever found in this country have been those of my own people.

Mrs Field was discharged a week later to a comfortable, friendly residential home. For his penance a couple of weeks later the consultant was rushed to theatre to have an appendicectomy.

I was visiting one of my patients at the hospital when a rather nervous junior doctor asked me if I would mind having a word with the consultant in the side ward about whether he would like the district nurse to remove his sutures on discharge, or would he be making his own arrangements. Now how could I refuse such a request?

'How kind of you to enquire,' he said, not bothering to glance up from his *British Medical Journal*. 'I shall probably go away somewhere for convalescence and get the nurse to remove them there.'

Seeing him sitting up in bed in his silver grey pyjamas with dark red piping, he looked vulnerable and I wondered why everyone was terrified of him. I couldn't resist having a little go at him while he was at a disadvantage and I had found the courage.

'If you haven't yet decided where to go for convalescence, sir, I know of an idyllic little house that's available. I took Sister O'Neil to see it the other day...'

He stared at me with a puzzled expression. Then it clicked. I do believe he blushed.

'I don't think I am quite that desperate for somewhere to stay.'

He looked thoughtful. 'But I think you've made your point.'

I walked towards the door. As I turned round to say goodbye, I could swear I saw him wink.

Chapter Fifteen

'What happen' to my dream, Mik? What happen' to that tall, rich, handsome guy in my dream? Poor Vern, he only pass on one count – you must agree, he is a good-looking guy.'

For all his shortcomings, Vernon adored Sarah, and she tended to fuss and mother him. I don't know if this is a familiar Jamaican trait or because he was five years younger. Occasionally he took a dominant stance then he grew in stature in her eyes and she loved him for it.

It was Vernon's birthday and we were having a party. Vernon and Sarah had been going together for a year. I thought back to when he first met Sarah and asked her to his firm's annual dance, and smiled to myself...

It was when Sarah had made a beautiful peacock blue taffeta dress for the occasion. She had tried it on and waited for me to comment. When I looked at her, there was an obvious human intervention, either that or a latent hormonal change had taken place. Sarah had suddenly sprouted large boobs. To be honest, not just large – enormous. I think Dolly Parton would be proud of them.

'How do I look?'

I gulped. 'Mm fine.'

'Are you sure?' she quizzed.

'Uh ha.' I nodded my head up and down vigorously trying not to explode with laughter.

Before Vernon had a chance to see the goods that she had now put in the shop window, she had wrapped herself in a matching stole. They went off happily together, hand in hand.

Halfway through the evening, as the band was preparing to break for a beer, Vernon was becoming more and more romantic, holding Sarah very close and whispering in her ear. The ripple of applause had stopped. The band was silent, their instruments put down, ready to go for a break. Couples were beginning to walk back to their seats. The silence was broken only by a man's loud voice exclaiming for all to hear, 'What the hell have I just touched on your back, girl? It's soft and spongy.'

One of Sarah's false boobs had broken loose and somehow worked its way around her dress to the centre of her back. Embarrassed by his outburst and discovery, she ran from the dance floor. She disappeared into the ladies' toilets, wrenched out the 'falsies' and threw them into the nearest bin. (No silicone implants then.) It took her an hour to summon up the courage to reappear and join Vernon.

Vernon thought the whole thing hilarious and teased Sarah all the way home.

'God, man, I thought I'd caught myself a jellyfish. I suppose you just wanted to get *abreast* of the other girls. Fancy you making a *boob* like that.'

I tried to calm her down. 'At least Vernon knows what he is getting now,' I said.

'You mean not getting.'

'Sooner or later he would have found out. You must admit it broke the ice.'

'Broke the ice, girl, it shatter it. He having second thoughts now.'

'He'll be back, you'll see,' I said.

Sarah was multi-talented, always bubbling with energy and enterprising ideas. When she wasn't sketching dress designs or cutting out material, she ran a catalogue. Her friends would call to look through the book or pay off some money. Thursday night she went to evening class for shorthand and typing. As soon as Sarah returned home, she would practise. Out would come the old Olivetti typewriter that Miss Harris had loaned her and she would commence.

Clack clack clack – clonk clonk clonk – tap tap tap ... *PING.* Hour after hour the quick brown fox was jumping over the lazy dog. There were times when I felt like kicking that lazy dog to get it to chase after the quick brown fox for a change. It was even worse when it was set to music. The monotonous noise droned on and on, hour after every pinging hour.

To break the monotony, she would change to shorthand with its bizarre language, *Pee, bee, tee, dee, chay, jay,* as she sat book in hand, chanting like some mystic.

One thing I most enjoyed was her cooking. Tasting the variety of Caribbean dishes more than made up for her more irritating hobbies, and it helped to make me far more adventurous with food.

Our staple diet was peas and rice. Dried red kidney beans were soaked overnight and when cooked with rice, the rice turned pink. At the time the only rice most of us ate was the pudding variety, except with curry. We didn't eat it as a vegetable.

With Sarah, we ate it with everything: salad with rice and peas, fish with rice and peas, chicken with rice and peas. Practically all savoury dishes were served with pink rice.

We had worked out a simple system for the division of labour by alternating the weeks to cook and clean. One week British food, the next Caribbean.

We set off to Brixton Market for some special food for the party. We were having curried goat with rice and maybe some mango. The fruit and vegetable stalls were bustling, not only with West Indians but people of different nationalities. Most were seeking the same thing, food to remind them of home. I suppose if I had been away from my home country for a few years and discovered cabbage or spinach in a foreign market place, it is faintly possible that I might feel homesick for these tasteless vegetables.

I noticed that most African immigrants were wearing their traditional dress. Sarah reckoned they would normally wear western dress, but considered themselves to be superior to West Indians and did not wish to be mistaken for them.

The market had some wonderful aromas, the acrid essence of citrus fruits, the distinctive woody scent of coconuts and the earthy smell of yams. Sarah lovingly picked up one of the ugliest-looking fruits I have ever seen. It was green and yellow, looking like an old man's bruised and wrinkled knee, but its unappetising appearance didn't put Sarah off and she bought two.

'Mik, don't go by the look of it. They're wonderful and sweet *and from Jamaica.*'

'Bit like yourself, then. You can't go by the look of you,' I joked. 'What do you call it?'

'Ugli fruit, and no jokes about the name,' she said, grinning.

I noticed she bought some huge emerald-green bananas about a foot long.

'They're plantain, they have to be cooked. We can have both for breakfast. The ugli fruit is a cross between a grapefruit and a tangerine and quite delicious. The plantain we can cook with bacon,' she said with excitement.

After the stall-holder had weighed her a pound of cornmeal she was then attracted by a slab of grey substance covered in white dust.

'The cornmeal I'm going to make into a thick yellow pancake that can be spread with jam or fruit.'

'And the grey block?'

'That's dried salt fish. I will have to soak it overnight and then it can be flaked off and made into flitters.'

The fact that we could easily buy fresh fish to make fritters, or flitters as she called them, was immaterial. It was the buying of familiar foods that reminded her of home that was more important.

Coming out of the market, we were stopped by a young man with long hair worn in dreadlocks selling home-made jewellery and wooden sculptures. His stall was on the pavement on the main street. As he drew closer, the hair gave off a pungent odour similar to a fat Turkish cigar. The mane of unkempt stringy spirals dusted the jewellery as he moved. He wore a black knitted hat with red, green and yellow stripes.

As soon as he spoke his style of speech intrigued me. He kept saying I and I for everything. He seemed to replace *me*, *we* and *mine* with I and I. He said he was from one of the tribes of Israel and that he was exiled from his true land of Ethiopia.

'Why Ethiopia?' I asked him. His accent was distinctly Jamaican.

'The Black King is the Redeemer,' he said. I became more curious. 'Who do you mean?' I asked.

His well-rehearsed response, rolled off his tongue. 'Emperor Haile Selassie, Ras Tafari Conquering Lion of the Tribe of Judah, Elect of Jah and King of Kings of Ethiopia. I and I mean God is in all men.'

'Yes I see,' I said. There didn't seem much more I could add to that.

'Our doctrines...' he went on.

'Mik, come on.' I felt Sarah tug at my coat. She whispered, 'you do *not* want to hear this.' There was an urgency in her voice that my instinct told me to move on quickly.

'Who are these *I and I* people?' I asked her.

'They're Rastas, they use ganja – marijuana. It sends them crazy and fills them full of weird ideas. They believe they are the reincarnations of the ancient tribes of Israel and that the white man has kept them in exile. Girl, they have lots of strange doctrines.'

'Such as?' I persisted.

'One of their doctrines is to hate the white race,' she said.

As all this conversation was taking place on the top of a bus full of white people, I decided to drop the subject for the time being.

I helped Sarah prepare the curried goat for the party. Sarah had made something special for Vernon, mannish water, a soup that was said to be an aphrodisiac and given to bridegrooms on their wedding night.

'What is so special about mannish water?'

'Its secret ingredient.'

'What *is* the secret ingredient?'

'Ah, it wouldn't stay a secret if I told you,' Sarah teased. 'It's a certain part of goat.'

'Which part?'

She laughed. 'The testicles, of course. I could have given him cow cod soup, that has the same ingredients.'

'What's the difference then?'

'Oh, there's a *big* difference, girl. It's a lot bigger, it come from a bull.'

'Hold on, you'd better let me know when you intend giving him that, and I'll make sure to take off for the weekend,' I quipped.

After I had wished Vernon the usual felicitations, I thought I'd ask him about the Rastafarians.

'I think they are harmless enough, Mik,'

he said. 'I don't know what they like in Jamaica. Sal would know more about that.'

'They all wear the same type of coloured hats, are they symbolic?' I asked him.

'Their tam, yeah. Each colour has a meaning, black the colour of the skin, red the blood of the people, green for the homeland of Ethiopia and gold represent hope of being freed from the white man. Most of the reggae guys are Rastas. But those "dreads", gee man, they grow like tapeworms. I only go to barber once in two year. If I left my hair more than two year, it would start to break off. It must be the holy herb that they take as part of their religion,' he said with a smile.

'I remember my father telling me one of the leaders got himself arrested for preaching against the government,' said Sarah.

Later that week Sarah was in for a shock, when *she* was arrested. She was in a large departmental store called Le Bon Marché in Brixton and had spent a few minutes choosing a reel of bright pink cotton. She left the shop and was walking along the road when a policeman put his hand on her shoulder and stopped her.

'Where do you think you're going?' he said in a gruff voice.

'What's wrong?' she asked.

'I have reason to suspect that you have

185

stolen some garments from the Bon Marché store.'

'I am the store detective,' said an officious-sounding woman.

'Is this the suspect?' asked the policeman.

'What are you talking about, suspect? I haven't done anything,' Sarah protested.

'I am arresting you on suspicion. You had better come to the station with me. Give me your name.'

'I'm not telling you my name and I'm not going anywhere, I haven't done anything.'

'I want to look in your shopping bag,' said the policeman.

He fingered through some onions, a pineapple and a reel of cotton. Eventually she agreed to go back to the shop. The policeman and the store detective escorted her to the manager's office. By now Sarah felt humiliated and was very angry. She was also worried that a colleague or a patient might have seen her being marched back to the shop. People in the street stopped and gawped at she passed by with the police officer.

The store detective told her story in the manager's office.

'Two people shouted out that they had seen someone steal a couple of leather jackets. They pointed to her,' she said, directing her finger towards Sarah.

'But I haven't taken anything,' said Sarah,

beginning to get upset.

'Just a minute, we'll hear your story later,' said the policeman.

'I followed her down the street,' the store detective continued, 'and watched her buy a pineapple and some onions, then she looked in a gift shop window.'

'Miss Brown,' said the manager, 'are you saying that you left the shop and followed this woman?'

'Yes I did,' she said, with a grin of satisfaction.

'Good job she did,' said the policeman.

'Not at all, officer, said the manager. 'She is not supposed to leave the store.'

'Yes I know, but in the circumstances–' the policeman began.

'In the circumstances, as I see it,' said the manager, 'by so doing she allowed the thieves to get away with the goods. This young woman was used as a decoy. Mrs MacKay, on sundries, saw two men run out of the shop seconds beforehand, bundling what looked remarkably like black leather goods into a bag. The two people who called out were probably part of a gang.'

The policeman looked uncomfortable and said, 'Well, I just acted on the telephone call.'

Miss Brown blushed and muttered, 'They're never satisfied here.'

'Please sit down,' said the manager to

Sarah. 'I'll get someone to bring you some tea. I'm really sorry about all this. I'm afraid we have all been a bit too hasty.'

'I don't think you would have been quite so hasty if I was white,' said Sarah angrily. 'I will be taking this matter further.'

'Come now, I don't think there is any need to take that attitude,' said the manager.

'Calm down now, a mistake was made. That's all there is to it,' said the policeman.

'It is *not* all there is to it. I have been wrongly accused, frogmarched up the street and made to feel like a criminal.'

'I think I had better take you home,' said the policeman.

'I'm not going to be seen in a police car,' said Sarah.

'No, I'll take the lady home,' said the manager.

The manager arrived home with Sarah, accompanied by the police officer. Vernon was on the sofa drinking tea when they walked in.

'What happening, man?' said Vernon, agitated.

Sarah didn't wait for the men to explain. Tears cascaded down her cheeks.

'Ve ... r-rnon Ve ... rr-nnon...' she sobbed. 'I've been arrested.'

Vernon put his arm around her, to comfort her. 'What have you done to her?' he shouted.

'There's been a mistake,' they both said.

'What, my girl say you arrest her and you say it's a mistake? Man, this going to be some costly mistake, you ain't getting away with this.' Vernon was livid. He was so angry I thought he was going to take a swing at them both. 'You don't treat people like this. My girl is in nursing, she's a midwife.'

The policeman scribbled in his notebook but remained silent. The manager cleared his throat and straightened his tie.

'Naturally I am very sorry, the Bon Marché store will wish to make amends. I will be making out a full report. There will of course be some form of compensation.'

After the men had gone, Sarah explained what had happened. 'The cheek, the manager wanted to fob me off with a voucher,' she said.

'How much for?' I asked.

'Twenty-five pounds. I don't care about the money, it's the principle.'

'Still, it's lot of money,' said Vernon.

Two days later a formal apology arrived from the store, together with the voucher.

'Listen here, girl, if you think for one minute I'm going in that lousy shop... What do they think I am? After the way they treat me like a thief, I won't be using no voucher.'

'Don't be silly, you may as well spend it,' I said.

'Monika, I'm serious. I'll never go in that

shop again, do you hear, never, NEVER, NEVER. I shall send it back. They can stick their voucher up their arrh ... their – *rectum*, for all I care.'

Two weeks before Christmas, Sarah sneaked into the shop and spent the voucher.

Chapter Sixteen

Martha was seventy-four and had been a widow for five years. She had been a diabetic for many years and her husband used to give her her insulin. After he died, she lost her confidence and depended on the district nurse.

Martha was lonely. I asked her if she had ever thought of taking in lodgers.

'Oh no, you never know who you might get,' she said. 'Could be a rough old lot. Perhaps a lady would be all right, but I would never be able to sleep with a man in the house.'

'How about a policeman?'

Tony had mentioned to me that they were looking for decent accommodation for three police cadets.

'Ah well, that would be different. I'd feel safe then, wouldn't I?'

'It would be a bit of company for you and

a bit of extra cash,' I said. 'It wouldn't be too difficult, they have most of their meals at the canteen.'

Within two weeks the change in her was remarkable. David, the police cadet, had settled in and Martha was already fussing over him. It was lovely to see her so relaxed and smiling.

David was friendly and polite but immature. Already the uniform seemed to have gone to his head. A worrying aspect was confidentiality. He was overconfident, and when he talked of his involvement in solving crime, you would begin to wonder how the police force had managed without him for so long.

He was up early in uniform having breakfast. I gave Martha her injection and washed my hands. I picked up the clean hand towel that she had left out for me. Out of the corner of my eye I saw a huge black beetle in it. I let out a shriek and dropped the towel. David nearly choked on his toast and laughed loudly. I looked down at the floor to see that it was only a *joke* beetle. Another irritating practical joke of David's – it was his second one that week.

After he had left for work, I asked Martha if I could have a needle, thread and his pyjama bottoms. She looked at me, puzzled, then raised her eyebrows. I decided to get my own back and stitch up the bottoms of his pyjama legs. Unfortunately I was running late, so I grabbed them quickly. In my haste, I discovered too late afterwards, I had also sewn up his flies. I hurried on my way to visit my next patient, Annie.

At seventy-eight Annie was fit but had *enjoyed* ill health. Charles, her husband, had looked after her for years.

The previous year she was diagnosed with pernicious anaemia. She was delighted to have a genuine condition to latch on to. The district nurse went in regularly to give her vitamin B12 injections. Pernicious anaemia, despite the prefix, is curable and common. Before it was treatable, patients died. Sufferers, in an attempt to prolong their life, were required to eat raw liver.

Annie had wasted no time and had looked up the word *pernicious* in the dictionary. It had said *fatal*, and that was good enough for her. She now spent most of her time resting awaiting *the inevitable*, while her husband had wearily waited on her. That is, until he had collapsed with a stroke and was admitted to hospital. Now it was the district nurse's turn to dance attendance on Annie. The report from the hospital wasn't good. Charles had poor mobility and would need a great deal of care at home on his discharge.

The nurses had been going in more regularly, to help with Annie's personal care as well as her injections. It was no surprise to any of us to discover that when she was not aware she was being observed, she was able to adequately care for herself.

On my arrival I was surprised to see a cluster of people outside the front door.

The reason for the gathering was soon clear. A pungent, sickly smell of sulphur in Town gas was seeping through the letter box. For this to happen, gas would have had to come from the kitchen ... the whole house was full of poisonous gas. At that time, it would contain 15% carbon monoxide.

To my dismay, not one of the persons assembled looked as though they were actively doing anything.

'Has anyone tried to get in?' I asked anxiously.

'We haven't got a key,' said one.

'We can't break in,' said another.

'I'm a member of the Good Samaritans,' said one. 'We've been instructed that we are not allowed to break and enter without the police in attendance. I've telephoned the police and they are on their way.'

'Has anyone thought to ring for an ambulance?' I enquired. There was no response. 'Right, can one of you make yourself useful then and ring them,' I said sternly.

I looked around the huddled group and spotted a young lad of about thirteen. I called him over.

'I'll need some help. Come with me, I am *not* a member of the Good Samaritans, and we *are* going to break in,' I said angrily.

'You can't do that, you've got to wait,' said the woman.

'There is *no time to wait*, we are going in.'

We left them muttering among themselves.

'Just 'cos she's a nurse, she thinks she knows it all... Where's she taking Tim? I was told...' The Samaritan's voice tailed off.

I took Tim to the rear entrance. Together we helped each other scramble over the six-foot high fence and drop onto the concrete yard below.

'Take no notice of that lady, we are going to break open the back door. Who does she think she is anyway?' I muttered.

The boy smiled. 'My mum.'

If I told you that we heaved and struggled to open the back door, it would be a lie. The back door gave way easily, with the minimum of effort. Annie had planned to end her days in comfort. She had placed several cushions near the gas stove to alleviate any discomfort she might feel from the stone kitchen floor. A pillow had been placed in the oven itself, with the gas tap turned full on. This was at a time when gas *was* poisonous; today, although highly explosive, the gas is said to be innocuous when inhaled.

I immediately turned off the gas and

194

between us we managed to carry her through to the front room, where she had her bed. We opened all the windows. Somehow I expected the atmosphere to look hazy. The kitchen or the rest of the house didn't look any different, the air looked clear. But it's the smell that is unforgettable.

The neighbours thought that when the ambulance men arrived with her husband, Annie must have panicked and refused to open the door and the men had to take Charles back to the hospital.

Although Annie was unconscious, she was still breathing and had a pulse. The ambulance arrived first. As it drove away with the patient, the women on the doorstep were still arguing that we should have waited for the police and that we had acted illegally.

'Much longer and you would have had to phone for the undertaker,' I said.

When the police finally arrived, they apologised for having been delayed because of traffic. I gave them my statement and was about to go on my way, when I began to feel unwell. I felt dizzy and increasingly drowsy. I decided to cycle the mile back home, make myself a cup of coffee and try to stay awake. Carrying Annie through the gas-filled house had taken its toll. In the effort, I had inhaled a considerable amount of gas. I walked up and down the garden path, gulping in fresh air.

I remember putting the kettle on for coffee, then ... nothing. The next thing I remember were the porters wheeling me on a stretcher, oxygen mask on my face, taking me on the ward.

A woman opposite was groaning and shouting, 'Why did she have to interfere, why didn't she let me die?'

A nurse transferred me from the trolley to the bed and removed the oxygen mask.

The voice belonged to Annie.

As soon as I was settled in bed and the screens removed, to my astonishment, Miss Wright was at my bedside.

'If I had to place bets on which nurse would go for the heroics, it would be you. I have yet to meet a more accident-prone person. One minute you are breaking down someone's door, the next a nurse is having to break yours down,' said Miss Wright.

According to Miss Wright, I had telephoned the nursing office. I sounded drunk. The voice was so incoherent that Miss Wright was concerned and immediately sent one of the nurses to investigate. The nurse had to get the police to break open the door.

After a couple of days I was discharged home. I was able to return to work when the dizziness had gone and I could walk in a straight line. Once back at work, Martha was on my list for her insulin.

'No dear, young David has never mentioned anything to me about your little joke. Although my next-door neighbour saw him creep out early one morning and put what looked suspiciously like a screwed-up pair of pyjamas in the dustbin.'

Later that week, I was out with Tony and we saw Inspector Marshall coming out of the police station with David.

'Hallo, nurse, how are you?' asked David eagerly.

'I'm fine *now*, thanks,' I said, thinking that he knew I'd been in hospital.

'You want to keep an eye on her,' he said to Mike. 'She's a real wild one. The other morning she was at my place and couldn't wait to get her hands down the front of my pyjamas.'

I was stunned and angry. For once I couldn't think what to say. I was annoyed that he had embarrassed Tony in front of his boss. Tony looked ahead and walked on in stony silence. As soon as the two men were out of earshot, Tony turned on me. He was furious.

'What was that all about?'

I tried to explain, but he kept interrupting.

'I have been humiliated in front of my boss. And by a bloody cadet, of all people.'

'He was just trying to be clever. He was showing off. After all, it was only a joke.'

'A joke? Some joke! I shall be the joke. It

will be all around the nick tomorrow.'

'I'm sorry. How was I to know this would happen?'

Tony was fuming. Whenever I tried to explain, he would stop me in mid sentence. He became morose and refused to discuss it.

'This is childish,' I said. 'If you are going to ignore me for the rest of the evening, there doesn't seem to be much point in going to your cousin's for supper tonight.'

'Please yourself.'

'That's precisely what I will do.'

What had started out as a practical joke had seriously backfired. Tony refused to listen to any explanation. 1 said goodnight and crossed over the busy street to the taxi rank.

'These men are great at giving the jokes, but they can't take them,' said Sarah. 'They can take it from a man but never from a woman. If they think a woman has got one over on them, it bruise their ego. It's all to do with saving face in front of other men. All that time we spend massaging men's fragile egos. Why do we bother, girl?'

'It was worse because it was in front of his boss,' I said.

'In the end it only show they not as tough as they think they are. This guy of yours, he get upset. A policeman? Man, he better toughen up.'

I went into the kitchen and decided to write him a letter. This was not the first time that he had behaved like this. The waste paper bin soon began to fill up with torn and crumpled letters.

I penned a one-liner... It was all over.

Sarah came back in the kitchen, looked at my face and got out the bottle opener.

Chapter Seventeen

Hela didn't seem to mind going into rat-ridden houses or working in filthy conditions. She even pointed out bed bugs to me, which I hadn't recognised as such, and other bugs that were under peeling wallpaper. Hela was a tall well-built girl originally from Poland. She was an excellent, hard-working, dedicated nurse. No task or situation perturbed her. We quickly struck up a friendship.

'It doesn't seem to bother you, Hela, going into dirty dilapidated homes,' I said to her one day.

'No, it doesn't,' she said. 'Probably because I have seen a lot worse than this.'

'Worse than this, where?' I asked.

'In the death camps, I was in Auschwitz,' she said calmly. 'Apart from Miss Wright, I haven't told anyone here.'

Hela found it difficult to trust people. She said she found it hard to make friends and confide in anyone.

I didn't ask her about Auschwitz. I felt she would tell me in her own time if she needed to. During the time that we worked together, little by little she unfolded her life. Sometimes it would be the odd remark, another time it would be page by page.

She told me she was seventeen when she was released by the Russians in 1945.

'Would you ever go back to Poland?' I asked.

'No, it wouldn't be the same now. Besides, I have no family there, they were all killed.'

She began to tell me about the ghetto in Poland.

'They walled off a section of the town and where I lived there were still one or two factories. We didn't have a proper school for the children but there were teachers who gathered a few children together and gave them some lessons. The rations became less and less and people began to die of malnutrition. My father and brother were still able to work but they had to exist on meagre rations.'

The food that she described for the workers only amounted to about 700 calories a day. The rest of the family, she said, had less than that.

'We heard shootings taking place all the

time. Killing was an everyday event. People got used to hearing screams and cries and shots and just thanked God that they were still alive. My father was taken very ill and he later died of tuberculosis and starvation. My brother was deported and died in Sobibor. I was fourteen when I was deported with my mother and Anna, my sister, to Auschwitz. Anna was only six. We got separated shortly after we arrived.

'We were petrified of Auschwitz. We knew it was a death camp. The black smoke, the giant fire, the smell ... the smell of burnt flesh. After a while I suppose we got used to it. That is not to say I can forget it. It was a smell I shall never forget. My mother and sister I never saw again. They went to the gas chambers.'

As she recalled this harrowing time, her voice was flat, devoid of all emotion. Emotion was a feeling that she had been forced to repress for many years.

One morning when Hela borrowed my enema apparatus she said it was for a lady on her list who had also survived a concentration camp. Because of ill treatment, the patient had lost all bowel function and needed to have repeated enemas.

'I was forced to have treatment to stop my menstrual cycle. I shall never be able to have my own children,' said Hela. She was only thirty-two.

It was the week of the practical examinations. This meant that along with five other colleagues, including Hela, we would have the Queen's Nursing Examiner to accompany us on our rounds for one morning. Sarah had arrived three months before me and had passed hers already. The day before, I checked each patient on my list to make sure all the equipment was ready and that the patients were primed.

'Don't get in a flap, nurse. I'll tell her what a terrible nurse you are,' teased one of my regulars. 'I'll tell her what happens when you put the newspaper on the floor and the bowl of water on it to wash my feet. You start washing my feet then something catches your eye in the newspaper and the washing and drying goes into slow motion,' she said, laughing.

The patients were hand picked by the Superintendent, eliminating the lousy households, so at least it would be a scratch-free morning. Miss Wright had amended the list to include a leg ulcer dressing. Mrs Oxford had been slotted in. She was also the owner of Henry, who you will remember was noted for his preoccupation with ladies' underwear.

Henry was in fine form when I arrived and kept banging my leg with an empty enamel plate.

'Henry seems quite friendly today.' I said trying to reassure myself. 'I think he's trying to tell me he's hungry.'

'Come along nurse, we have no time for pleasantries this morning,' said the examiner sternly.

There was a technique for everything, especially for the Gladstone bag. I had been issued with a pocket-sized blue linen-backed book entitled, *The Queen's Institute of District Nursing: The Outline of District Nursing Techniques*, price 1s 3d. Like the students of Chairman Mao, who studied his little red book, I had studied and memorised the Queen's little blue book. With special reference to the Gladstone bag.

N.B. Place the bag on a clean surface. On *no account* place it on the floor.
1 Unfasten the lid.
2 Wash hands.
3 Take out the required articles.
4 Close the bag firmly.
5 Before and after use instruments to be sterilised.
6 Unfasten the lid of the bag again.
7 Wash hands.
8 Equipment to be thoroughly dried on a towel kept in the bag for this purpose and replaced.
9 Close bag.

The sterilisation took place in a pan of boiling water with two cups. The instruments were laid inside the cups, with the top of each cup facing each other. *The handles were left protruding out of the water.* To make sure that everything stayed in position a saucer was wedged at the side. Then, like hard-boiled eggs, they were boiled for five minutes. Once they were cooked, *holding both handles* and cupping the instruments inside, I had then to manoeuvre the cups onto a clean dressing towel on the table.

This was no mean task and was guaranteed to convey the sterilised equipment in a hundredth of a second. Whoever dreamed this one up, stating that *the handles would not be so hot as they were not immersed in the boiling water*, should have been made to test out this procedure for a day. I would like to have seen that person take the steaming equipment with bare hands and safely place it on the table without grimacing or swearing.

Having performed this operation on a daily basis over a long period of time, I must say it has given me an unrivalled skill when having a meal in a restaurant. When the waiter, with his asbestos gloves, hands me a plate straight from the furnace, I am able to smile and accept it without a murmur or even a slight wince.

The dressings had to be made by hand, with the patient usually supplying a biscuit tin in which to sterilise them, and baked in the oven with the lid left loose. The dressings would usually sit alongside a rice pudding and cook in a moderate oven for one hour. Like the rice pudding, the colour of the dressings was supposed to be a golden cream, but it depended on what was cooking. If it happened to be a Christmas cake, then you could expect the dressings to turn out the same colour.

How different today, with patients able to get their own sterile pack on prescription, or the district nurse pick up her dressing pack from the health centre with its five swabs, five square gauze dressings and surgical instruments. Some packs have sterile rubber gloves as well.

I was becoming quite nervous under the scrutiny of the examiner, The removal of the soiled dressing was a work of art. I would have to remember to keep one pair of forceps for the clean dressings and another for the dirty ones. Then the dirty dressings had to be placed in a Queen's paper bag.

This was where I had to try my hand at origami with a sheet of newspaper. If it was done properly, when turned upside down it would remind you of Uncle Jim's Christmas hat from *Blue Peter*. The Dettol solution in the jar would be waiting for the dunking of the dirty forceps. One of my looming worries, that I was trying hard not to think about, was Henry. How was I going to be able to perform correctly without bending down? I knew this dog, and at the first sign of a curtsey ... he'd have me.

Henry's owner, remembering the knicker-tearing episode last time, had taken the precaution of having the dog firmly clasped on her lap. That was, until I bent down to remove the dressing from her leg. The band-age needed to be unwound slowly as the stained dressing appeared to have adhered to her leg.

As I continued to gently unwind the band-age to remove the dressing, Henry growled. He started with his basso profundo then he swiftly moved up the scale to castrato. Castrato was the operation I could cheerfully have performed on him that day.

He shivered and shook. His teeth kept going up and down like an Austrian blind. Suddenly he was in flight and made to bite my hand as I unravelled the bandage. Instead he tore at the bandage and began a game of tug of war. The dressing finally freed, he ran around the room with his 'prize', a length of bandage and an infected pus and blood soaked dressing. To the dis-gust of us all, but especially the examiner.

Mrs Blanc was my next visit with the exam-iner, a friendly little French lady who thoughtfully had everything waiting for me.

She insisted on interrupting the proceedings with unhelpful comments such as, 'I've made sure everything is clean *this* time, nurse.'

'Thank you Mrs Blanc.'

'I don't *normally* change the surgical spirit in the jar so often, but I've changed it *again* for you so it is all right for your exam!'

When I first visited Mrs Blanc she took delight in telling me about a lodger she had during the Second World War.

'He was a real gentleman. Always polite. Very smart. He didn't entertain any ladies, he was very proper,' she told me. 'Sometimes men would arrive at night, with little black boxes and go to his room for a meeting.'

She took me into what would have been the room where he held his secret meetings. I was intrigued.

'One Saturday night when he came home he had blood on his face and his clothes were torn. I asked him what had happened. He brushed the incident aside and said that he had got involved in a bit of a scuffle. I could see it was more than that and I offered to bathe his cuts and bruises. He said he was fine and that he could do that himself.'

'What had happened?' I asked, becoming curious.

'He wouldn't say, then shortly after, I was at the cinema with my friend and there he was on the newsreel – Oswald Moseley leading the Fascists in their black shirts.'

'What became of him after that?'

'That day he had come down to breakfast, thanked me and put two weeks' rent on the table. When I got back from the cinema he wasn't in. In the evening he didn't return. I went upstairs and looked in his wardrobe. Everything had gone and so had he. I never saw him again. He had been interned – that was in 1940. He was supposed to be in prison for the duration of the war but they let him out earlier because of ill health.'

Oswald Mosley had been a Member of Parliament and was the founder of the British Fascist Movement. After the war it was discovered that Italy had funded the Fascist organisation in Britain. Two years later he revived the movement.

Surprisingly, despite various mishaps, I managed to scrape through my practical exam.

Later that week Hela had her practical. Miss Wright had briefed the examiner as to her background. She had failed twice before due to her extreme nervousness and inability to concentrate when being questioned.

Miss Wright had asked the examiner to go easy on her. But as soon as the examiner started to ask her any questions, she went to pieces. Afterwards she said that when she was questioned she experienced flashbacks from her time when she had been interrogated.

I was upset to learn that Hela had failed

her practical exam and that this was her last chance. What a loss to the service of such a caring and conscientious person, simply because she couldn't hold it together for the duration of the practical examination. Why couldn't there have been a more sensitive arrangement, adapted to take her problem into consideration?

Hela said goodbye and left the Queen's. I was not the only one that was upset for her. There were very few dry eyes to be seen that day. Miss Wright surprised us all. She hugged her and kissed her goodbye. I saw her openly weeping, before hurriedly disappearing to her room.

Chapter Eighteen

'Are you hurt? Stupid idiot, what the hell was he thinking about? Here, let me help you.'

Through a dark blue fog, shapes began to form and voices that were once distant and echoing were beginning to become audible.

'Where am I?' I asked.

'She looks dazed,' said the second man.

'So would you look dazed after what you've just done. You fool, you could have killed her.' said the man in the blue uniform.

I tried to make out the uniform; it wasn't dark enough for the police. Both the men's faces were blurred.

'I *always* look in my mirror,' I heard the second man say.

'You didn't look this time. Ah, here's the ambulance ... at last,' said the uniformed man. Firm hands wrapped me in a blanket and lifted me on to a stretcher and into the ambulance. I wanted to speak but no sound emerged from my lips.

'I think she's trying to say something,' said a woman sitting beside me.

'Perhaps she wants a drink?'

I felt my lips moistened with water as my body swayed with the movement of the vehicle. The rear doors opened and I could make out the words *Casualty Ambulances Only*. The porters swiftly transported me through the swing doors.

'Are there any witnesses?' asked Sister.

'Yes, the driver of the car, Mr Cardinal, he's following in his own car,' said the ambulance woman.

'The lorry driver?' Sister enquired.

'The police have detained him, Sister.'

The sister turned to me and in a gentle voice said, 'You'll be all right now. After you have seen the doctor, we'll be taking you to the ward. What is your name?'

I went to answer and, to my astonishment, I couldn't remember.

'What's happened?' I asked, bewildered.

This was my worst nightmare. I thought I must be dreaming and would wake up and my headache would be gone and I would be in my own bed.

'Don't worry, don't try to remember at the moment. It will come back shortly,' said Sister.

Sarah said she came that evening. I had no recollection of her visit, nor that of Miss Wright.

A man called, in his RAF uniform, and one of the nurses brought him over to my bed.

'Your boyfriend is here to see you. That will cheer you up.'

Boyfriend? I don't recognise this man at all? What do I say to him? This is terrible, I thought.

'Don't look so puzzled. I'm Roy, but I don't expect you to remember me,' said the handsome man in uniform. 'I'm afraid it was my car that you hit, when you had your accident.'

'Oh! I see.' I sighed with relief. 'I'm sorry, I can't remember what happened.'

'You were catapulted from outer space like a UFO,' he said. 'One minute I was turning the ignition and starting to move off, then you did a nose dive and came to land on the top of the bonnet.'

Slowly the picture emerged. Although I still couldn't remember my name, or what I was doing, I did recall cycling past a stationary lorry.

'The driver opened his cab door, which must have been level with you as you cycled past. He forgot to look in his wing mirror,' said Roy. 'I can't stay, I have to go back to camp tonight at Leamington. Would you like me to write to you and see how you are getting on?'

'Thank you, that's kind of you – except I can't give you my name and address at the moment.'

'I already have it, I got it from Sister for my insurance company. Goodbye, Monika, good luck,' he said, and was gone.

He seemed a pleasant young man about my age, tall with dark hair and a tanned complexion. At least he showed some concern by visiting me. Or was it just to get details from the ward sister for his insurance claim?

I looked around the room. I was in a two-bedded side ward. In the other bed was a woman in her thirties who had been to theatre that day. She was still wearing a theatre gown and had a blood transfusion in progress.

Sister came in and checked the woman's transfusion and mentioned that she would be coming back to give me an injection later for pain. I tried to sleep; houses and names were reeled in front of me, then weddings and husbands. I awoke sweating. Had I got a husband? Just imagine if I had a husband and I couldn't recognise or remember him. The more I chewed over these questions, the fewer the answers. I drifted in and out of sleep.

In the morning, I awoke to find my room companion with her drip removed and sitting up in bed. Piece by piece my memory was stirring, although the incidents prior to the accident on that day remained a blank.

My memory took a serious kick-start when I recognised who was in the next bed. It was Ruth, the young woman who was living in comfort in the flat above her father's basement hovel.

At first she didn't recognise me. I offered her water when she was thirsty and mopped her forehead with a face cloth to cool her down. Suddenly she opened her eyes.

'What are *you* doing here?' she said, staring at me.

'I'm in here as a patient myself,' I said. 'Are you all right? What happened to you?'

'I've lost the baby, I were three months gone.'

She started to get upset. I tried to comfort her.

'I'm sorry, I were very rude to you when you called at my house,' said Ruth.

'That's OK, it was a difficult situation for both of us,' I said. 'I am sorry about your baby.'

'I really wanted this baby for Paul's sake.'

'I'm sure you will have a chance to have another one,' I said.

She sobbed again and I put my arm around her.

'It brought it all back to me, having to go to theatre,' she said. 'This is not the first time I've had this operation. The first time I didn't really know what were happening, I were only fourteen and it were horrible.'

'You were very young, you must have been very frightened,' I said.

'It were a long time ago. I couldn't have kept it anyway.'

The orthopaedic consultant's round interrupted our conversation as he walked into the side ward with his entourage of medical students.

Ruth should have been on a gynaecological ward, but with the shortage of beds was put in a side ward.

'Good morning, how are you feeling?' he asked me.

'Fine thank you. A bit of chest pain, otherwise I'm OK.' On examination, I saw that I was covered in enormous bruises.

'You got off lightly with your escapade, young lady. Two fractured ribs and concussion,' said the consultant. He turned his attention to the students. 'Anything else anyone has noticed? Who has spoken to this lady?'

'I did, sir,' said a pimply youth, who looked just about old enough to join the Boy Scouts. It didn't exactly fill me with confidence, to think one day he would make life and death decisions.

'What did you notice?'

'Unequal pupils, sir.'

'Good. And...?'

'She has retrograde amnesia, sir.'

'Precisely,' said the consultant.

Ah well, it's amazing what they learn in the Scouts. Only two broken ribs, that's not bad. They would heal on their own and, apart from pain when I laughed, coughed, or breathed, I wasn't doing too badly. I should be home in a couple of days, I thought.

'Have you really lost your memory?' said Ruth after the consultant had gone.

'It's getting better all the time,' I said.

'Sometimes I wish I could lose my memory over certain things, just blot out huge chunks of my life.'

'This has happened through an accident, I haven't deliberately wanted to forget things.'

'Yeah I know. I were talking to your boyfriend yesterday. He said he were there when it happened.'

'Boyfriend, what boyfriend?' I asked.

'The one in the RAF. Wow! He is definitely *not* the sort of person I'd want to forget. He looks a good guy.'

'Oh, he's not my boyfriend, he's the fellow

whose car I apparently landed on.'

Ruth paused. 'You know, there is something I'd like to wipe out, I'm not proud of this, but when the old man used to come in roaring drunk, I'd always pray he would go to me mum first and leave me alone. I'd hear 'em fighting and I used to cover me ears with a pillow. At night, I still think I can hear Mum crying. *Leave me alone, stop it you drunken bastard*, she'd shout. *I don't give a shit what you want, you slut*, he'd yell back. He'd beat her up. In the morning me mum would look a mess. Why can't we get away from all this mum? I'd ask. *Ruthie*, she'd say, *I can't leave this place. I know it's not much, but it belonged to your granddad. I've had it all done legal so he can't get it. When I'm gone – it's yours.*

'Her friend Olive brought in a magazine one day, called *The Lady*, and showed her a job as a housekeeper for some posh people in the country. Me mum had never had a job, she were married at sixteen. *You could do that job*, said Olive to me mum. I know this sounds stupid, but I used to lie awake at night, imagining what it would be like. A large country mansion, red ivy on the walls, a remote village. No one would find us. Velvet curtains at the windows, not filthy, ripped cotton ones. Carpet fitted everywhere, ones that I could sink my feet into. No more bare floorboards and frozen feet.

Soft comfortable chairs. Plenty of chairs. We only had one chair.' Ruth spat the words out with contempt. *'His* chair.

'I were eleven when it happened. I came home from school. The cops was there, taking fingerprints. I screamed at them, where's Mum?'

'What had happened?'

'He'd killed her ... in the kitchen. They say she took a knife from the drawer to defend herself. He grabbed her and stabbed her. He went down for seven years for manslaughter. They sent me to a children's home. I ran away when I were fourteen.'

'Where did you go?'

'I went to stay with Iris, she were one of me mates at the home. Iris had a squat at the Elephant. At the back of the squat was a hotel. Iris showed me some rich pickings in the bins.'

'How could you survive like that?'

'Are you wanting me to spell it out? How do you think? Then one night, everything changed. I were at the hotel bins, when this chef caught me. He told me if I came back later, he would make sure I had a proper meal. Later I went back to the hotel. I thought he were going to give me a bag of food to take back. Instead, he asked me to go to his room – he lived in the staff quarters.

'On the table were chicken and chips. *Come on then sit down*, he says. When we'd finished he asked if I'd like to have a bath. Here we go, I thought. I put on his dressing gown and walked towards the bed.

'*What are you doing you can't stay here you'll get me the sack*, he says. I felt a fool, I thought you wanted something for the food. Then he says, *Ruth, put your clothes back on, I just wanted to give you a decent meal, that's all. I had no intention of taking advantage of you.*

'From then on we became friends. I used to call round to have a bath, watch TV, and when he finished his shift he would bring back two meals from the kitchens. Paul hated how I were living and in the end he got me a job washing up in the kitchens. I told him about my dad being sent down, and that he were out of prison now and probably back home.'

'But it wasn't your dad's house *now*, it was yours,' I reminded Ruth.

'Yeah, that's right, that's what Paul said. He said he would help me decorate and furnish it, and if I wanted him, he would share it with me. He told me not to have anything to do with me dad. Just pretend he's not there. It would be just him and me. We could have our own life. Then you came along.'

'What was it you said, Ruth? *I didn't live in the real world.* You were right, I didn't. I was trying to see it from your father's perspective. I had no idea what he had put you through or what you had suffered. You were quite right, Ruth, and I am sorry. I had no idea of *your world* at all.'

Chapter Nineteen

On my discharge from hospital and back home at the flat a letter awaited me, post-marked Leamington. Sarah watched for my reaction as I read it. I must have smiled as I put it back in the envelope.

'Mik, stop grinning like a clown and tell me what he said. Is he going to see you?'

'Huh huh.'

'You know I'm dying to know, what does he say?'

'Just that, he wants to see me,' I said, trying to appear indifferent.

'What do you think then, girl?'

'I might as well meet him I suppose,' I said.

'Is that it, you suppose?'

'I suppose I could say ... yippee,' I said with a grin.

Sarah gave a long sigh. 'Thank God for that, for a minute I thought you were going to pass up that handsome-looking hunk. Come on, Mik, let's see the letter. What does it say? I love you till the sands of the Sahara cease, or the River Nile runs dry?' she said, teasing, and made to grab the envelope.

'Go on, then,' I said, tossing her the letter across the table.

Hello Monika,
I hope your memory is returning and that you are not gazing at this letter bewildered as to who has written to you. I will be in London next weekend on a forty-eight-hour pass. Perhaps we could meet again, only this time in more pleasant circumstances.
Yours hopefully,
Roy Cardinal

'Mm,' said Sarah, 'not bad. Sounds keen. Oh, I nearly forgot, Miss Wright said she was going to send one of the nurses round to help you get washed and dressed,' Sarah added with an amused expression.

'Ha ha, I should think so, over my dead body,' I said.

'I said you would never agree but she insisted.'

There was a knock on the door and Sarah scampered to answer it.

'It's the nurse,' she announced, unable to keep from giggling.

I turned to see Ian Newton, the male nurse who I had sat next to on his first day. He stood blushing in the doorway, holding something behind his back. He walked over to the table and gave me a large bouquet of flowers.

'From the Queens' Nurses,' he said. He then held out a small paper bag. 'This is from me. I thought after your accident you might be needing it.'

I opened the package, and we both laughed. It was a tin of Cherry Blossom boot polish!

Male nurses were a recent innovation in district nursing although they had been around for some time in hospital. In the community they were more independent and liked the feeling of being their own boss with their round of male patients. We had two.

John Nicholson, the other male nurse, amused us with a tale of how he was sent to bath an eighty-five-year-old patient, Francis Boyd, only to find that he was a she, *Frances*. He apologised but she wasn't a bit perturbed.

'Don't worry if you can't do the bath, luv, just take me to the lav and help me get dressed,' she said, to his amusement.

'She was so insistent and I didn't know how to get out of it.'

Everyone liked John, a little round faced guy with mischievous eyes that looked like singed grass. Born at the turn of the century, he left school at fourteen and worked in a tannery, later becoming foreman. He saw action in World War II and would tell the tale of how he once removed the coat off a dead German officer.

'How horrible, I don't know how you could do that,' I said.

'Easy, Monika. He certainly didn't need it where he was going, and I felt a damn sight colder than he did.'

When he was evacuated from the beaches at Dunkirk in 1940, he had been helping to get men into the boats.

'I saw a young boy struggling in the water – he'd gone under twice. Come on, son, I said, I've got you. Amongst all the turmoil and tens of thousands of men, I couldn't believe it: I recognised him, he was one of the young lads from the tannery, underage, only fifteen.

'After I got demobbed I was unemployed, I said to my wife Carol, For two pins I'd go down the council and ask if they'd got any jobs. I don't care if it's on the bins. It was, and I got the job. With Carol expecting, I desperately needed work.

'I was nearing the end of my shift when my eye caught an advert in a newspaper for a hospital porter. It was the last day for applications so I hadn't a moment to lose. Despite being in my working clothes, which didn't exactly smell of lavender I knocked on Matron's door.

'*Come in*, she said. So I walked in. At the sight of me she screwed up her face in horror putting her handkerchief to her nose. *Little man,* she said. *Are you responsible for that terrible smell? No, NO, there's no need to come any closer. What do you want?*

"'I'm sorry Matron I've just come off the carts. You have a job advertised for a porter. I think I could do that."

'Do you? she said. *Come back washed and suitably attired and I may consider interviewing you.*

'I dashed home, washed and put on my demob suit and went back. I still laugh when I think about it. I must have smelt worse than last week's dirty nappy. Anyhow, I got the job. After I had been there a few years, I was watching the auxiliary nurses on the wards changing beds and making patients comfortable, getting them ready for X-ray and I went back to the matron and told her I thought I could do that. Eventually she let me have a go on a three-month trial.'

'How did you finally get qualified?' I asked him.

'There was this spread in the local paper about the opening of a new training school for nurses, so I applied. The matron was very off hand at first but eventually she let me sit the entrance exam and in six months I was in.'

He had been a staff nurse and a charge nurse and was well respected by his colleagues. The patients loved him he was always making jokes with them as well as teasing us. He was a great joker. When we were back at base, if Miss Wright rang from her office to the surgical room and we were in there together, he would delight in saying in an exaggerated whisper, 'Monika, get off my lap it's the boss on the phone.'

When it came to April Fools' day I would try to get my own back.

We had the road repairs in our street whilst the water board laid some new pipes, and I happened to come across some headed notepaper that one of the officials had dropped. It was a bit muddy, but there were several sheets that had been dropped, together with an official envelope. I immediately seized on them and took my prize home to show Sarah.

'Let's gently sponge the dirt off,' said Sarah, 'and then you can put a cloth over it and iron it.'

After I had done this, I was surprised how well it came out.

'Now all I need is to borrow Miss Harris's typewriter,' I said.

'I still have it here,' said Sarah.

After I had typed it we checked it through together.

'Yes, that looks official,' I said.

April 1st

Dear Mr Nicholson,
Recently we undertook a survey in your

district and we were alarmed that you had exceeded your quota of 12 gallons per head of household. In these economic times it is essential that each citizen acts responsibly to conserve water. One of the methods that you can cooperate with, is by stricter use of the water closet. It is suggested that you restrict yourself to only flushing the toilet thirteen times each day.

I trust that I shall not have to draw your attention to this matter again.

Yours sincerely,
Eva Binhadd

When John came in with the letter, he was furious. He was going to ring the water board. He had misunderstood the letter and started moaning, 'Damn cheek, who do they think they are? You know me, girls. I go to the toilet here most of the time, or in the community. I'm sure Carol doesn't use any more water since she retired. I'll wait until nine o'clock and then I'll ring this Binhadd woman.'

Miss Wright put her head round the door. 'I have a call from your wife, Mr Nicholson. It sounds urgent – you can take it in my office.'

When he came back in the room his face had reddened. 'Carol just rang. She reminded me what day it was. You little devils, I'll get my own back.'

He put his hand in his pocket and pelted us with a handful of mint imperials.

John lived with his wife Carol in a two up, two down terraced in Camberwell.

'I don't need anything any bigger. It suits us two now that Bryan's got married and left home.'

One patient in particular held him in great admiration and had every reason to be grateful to him. John had walked in to find Mr Rees choking on a fish bone. Instinctively he thumped him between his shoulder blades as he turned blue then white and stopped breathing. His pulse had gone. He took out a pair of forceps from his case and just managed to hook out the offending bone and then gave him mouth to mouth resuscitation. With a sudden cough and to the relief of them both, he started breathing again. Their photograph featured in the local paper, with the gentleman holding up the offending fish bone.

Mr Rees kept asking him if he would take some money, but he refused, saying that he was happy enough to see him alive and well, that was payment enough.

'You're a stubborn man. If you won't have it now, I'll leave you something when I go.'

'I don't need anything,' said John.

'That doesn't come into it. If it wasn't for you, I wouldn't be here now,' said Mr Rees. 'I'm going to leave you the bungalow. My kids in Australia don't want it, they both have big houses in Adelaide. My mind's made up. In fact I'll ring my solicitor today.'

Mr Rees's bungalow was in a pleasant area in Streatham. The following day when John got there, the Doctor was writing out a certificate and was handing it to a neighbour. Mr Rees had had a massive heart attack and died in the night.

John walked into the sitting room to collect his nursing notes. On the table in the centre of the room were laid out all Mr Rees's legal documents ready for his solicitor, who was coming over that morning.

John attended his funeral and met Mr Rees's two sons who had flown over from Australia.

'We don't know what we'll do with his bungalow,' said one. 'We don't want it, we will probably put it up for sale. Or we might keep it in case one of us decides to come back to England.'

John often passed the neat little bungalow with its manicured lawns and shrubs. It did not take long for it to look dowdy and unkempt. After a couple of years the gardens were untamed and attracted bottles and other rubbish. Kids used to climb over the fence and some had lit a bonfire. Neither did it take long before the squatters moved in.

'What a waste,' John sighed. 'If only...'

Chapter Twenty

Roy was waiting for me at the Tudor Tea Rooms at Dulwich village. He had driven from early morning and was still in his RAF uniform. I had told him about our cockney waitress at the tea rooms and he decided that this would be an ideal place to meet. He ordered coffee and cakes. Unfortunately he wasn't able to share in the joke as our favourite waitress was off duty.

The customers seemed busy gossiping and drinking tea. The RAF uniform soon attracted attention, with people twisting and craning their necks to get a better view. As if that wasn't sufficient, when Roy spoke, the tea rooms became silent. Roy had their undivided attention.

'The last time I saw you, Monika, you were in bed with that hideous nightdress on.' Eyebrows raised, ears strained for a response. 'How are you feeling, now that you are out of hospital?'

Stifled giggles, and customers resumed their conversations.

Blushing, I told him that I felt fine and was back to work.

'How about you, how long have you been

in the RAF?'

'I went in as a boy entrant when I was nearly sixteen. My first job was packing parachutes. It may not sound much, but it was a responsible job. As you can imagine, it was just a trifle important that the chute opened properly and at the correct time of descent.'

We walked out of the tea rooms. Roy slipped his hand into mine as we crossed the road to where he had parked his car. My heart raced for a couple of seconds, but I quickly dismissed it as indigestion, thinking how foolish I was to have eaten a second doughnut.

'Where would you like to go?' Roy asked.

'You decide,' I said.

'What about Madam Tussaud's?'

We agreed it would be a good place to go as the weather was unsettled.

'We'll go back to my place, leave the car and go by bus and tube to Baker Street.'

I guessed the real reason behind this was for me to meet his mother.

Mrs Cardinal greeted me warmly. They lived in a large bay-windowed house in Thurlow Park Road in a pleasant leafy district between Tulse Hill and West Dulwich.

'My son tells me you were very lucky not to get killed and that he took you to the hospital.'

'Yes, I was very lucky. Roy was very kind.' Roy glanced at me and grinned.

The sitting room smelled of fresh paint. There was a vase of yellow chrysanthemums and their distinctive spice-like perfume lingered in the room. On the piano near the window was a framed photograph of what I took to be Roy's father in RAF uniform. He was killed during the war, when Roy was only two years old. Tall, with brown expressive eyes, his father made a handsome figure.

We were about to leave when a well-built man walked in from the kitchen. I recognised him as George, a well-known character in the area. A man of an indiscernible age, with a learning disability, he was frequently in the local library. He spent most of his time in the children's section. It was indicative of Roy's character that not only had he time for someone whom I knew to be shunned by society, but that he actively encouraged him to visit.

'I'm sorry, George. As you can see, I have company today. Perhaps we can have a chat another time.'

George looked anxious. 'This your girlfriend?'

Roy turned his palms over, shrugged, and looked across at me, eyebrows raised. He smiled. 'You could be right, George.'

Before the pill and the sexual revolution, romance deliberately took a very slow pace and could be fraught with anxiety. Its progress must seem very tame to the youth of today. Now, friends might quiz, Did he score? (as though it's only a game) or, Did you have sex with him? Any hint of a romance is sacrificed, for a single clinical sexual act.

But in the early sixties, a fellow would be asked by his mates... How far did you get? Did you kiss her? Petting was the expression of the day, divided into light and heavy. Quite where the dividing line was I don't know. Despite the male hormones erupting like Mount Vesuvius, *heavy* petting was generally seen then as the ultimate aim. I suspect that most decent men worried about getting a girl pregnant.

As for the girl, it dominated every relationship with the opposite sex. A girl would monitor any tactile progression with apprehension as to where it would lead to and how and when to shut up shop.

The stigma then for an unmarried girl to become pregnant was heaped on with a shovel. Loss of respect headed the list, for the girl and her family. Fathers would warn sons, Don't bring any trouble into our house. Or, as I once heard crudely said, 'No good you thinking you're bringing her in here, with a belly full of arms and legs!' Babies were snatched for adoption or illegally aborted. Someone always knew for a price where to go to get rid of it. Not always successfully. Myths and advice were readily available, most of them unsuccessful:

1 You can't get pregnant if you were standing up at the time.
2 Jump up and down afterwards.
3 Drink a bottle of gin and have a hot bath.
4 The bark of a slippery elm. (Strips of bark were inserted into the vagina to dilate the cervix.)
5 Hot carbolic douche.

Babies that were kept were sometimes passed off as belonging to the married one in the family, or the girl's mother, having 'had one in the change'.

At that time anyone who kept and looked after their baby deserved admiration as they would often be ostracised by the entire community and their child taunted at school as a bastard. Nurses were often asked if we knew how to get rid of a baby.

In front of his mother and George, Roy took my hand, squeezed it and led me out of the front door. We held hands as we walked to the bus stop.

The underground was packed. It was half-term school holiday, and there was standing room only. As the train drew into the busier stations the passengers were churned out onto the platform whether they wanted to or not, and had to scramble back in again before the doors automatically closed.

After being yanked in the wrong direction twice, I tried to hold on tight to Roy's hand. This time the hand felt different, rough as sandpaper and cracked.

'Whose hand have I got hold of here?' I called out.

A deep voice croaked in the crowd, 'Mine.'

A young Australian man strap-hanging remarked in a loud voice, 'Good on yer, Grandad,' and the passengers chuckled.

After making a fool of myself at the waxworks, by asking the *wax* security guard where I would find the chamber of horrors, we walked to Regents Park and the Zoo. It was my turn then to laugh at Roy when an elephant decided to unload the contents of his trunk, splattering some green foul-smelling liquid down his uniform.

We stopped off on the way back for a drink at a large hotel and sat in the comfortable lounge. Conversation was easy as Roy had a good sense of humour and friendly person-ality. Although we couldn't see the bar we could see a waiter darting about serving drinks at other tables.

After some considerable time, Roy became agitated, having several attempts to attract the waiter's attention. Other patrons had drifted in and out.

'Do you intend to serve us?' he said when a waiter passed close to our table. The waiter ignored him. Roy knew it would bring a swift response, so he whistled him. At this, the waiter appeared immediately at our table with a look of contempt on his face.

'We only serve *officers* in uniform here, and please do not whistle again.'

Perhaps the odour from the zoo had something to do with it. Unperturbed, we made our way to a pub nearer home.

Hardly had Ray brought the drinks back to the table, when the pub was hit by a power cut. The landlord being away, it was left to the barman to cope. He eventually produced three candles: one for the till, one for the bar, and the other, he placed on one of the tables in the centre of the pub.

Customers joined in the spirit of things and started singing, *When the lights go on again all over the world* and other wartime tunes.

There was one problem. If anyone wanted to go to the lavatory, it would mean that person taking the candle with them, plunging the main area of the pub into darkness. Any thought of nipping off to the toilet unnoticed was out of the question. I waited as long as hygienically possible, before having to make my silent announcement to everyone in the pub the reason why the pub would be in darkness.

The barman came forward and removed the candle and asked me to put my hands around his waist, *he* would guide me there.

We moved off as though we were about to dance the conga.

Of course it was not completely dark as the customers could map my journey across the pub and down the corridor by watching the disappearing candle.

A scream went up as a pint of best bitter landed in someone's lap and a chair clattered to the floor. A loud slurred voice shouted, 'If someone wants to take the candle they should announce it, I say, not just leap up and grab it. And we'd all stop drinking.'

'Huh, we would, would we?' came a woman's voice. 'I'd like to see that day, Billy Bennett, when you put *your* glass down for a minute and stop drinking,' she said, to the amusement of the customers in the darkened pub.

Chapter Twenty-one

I looked in all directions at the busy traffic at Camberwell Green and the quiet little slip road that I had always used to Peabody Buildings, and decided to take a chance. True, the *No Entry* sign had been there for a couple of weeks, but I couldn't see any harm if no one was using the road and, more to the point, I couldn't see a bobby anywhere.

A booming voice vibrated in my ear; I suspect its owner had crouched behind the thick bush on the corner of the slip road. 'Stop! Where the bloody hell do you think you're going?'

Oh no – it *would* be the same policeman that caught me last time, with his *Next time I won't be so lenient.*

'Nurse, do you realise you're trying to cycle down a one-way street? Aren't you the nurse I spoke to before about this?'

'Sorry, can't stop, I have a delivery,' I said in an anxious voice.

'Oh! I see. Well, that's different. Quick, nurse, I'll guide you through.'

He leapt out into the road and put his broad gloved hand up to stop any oncoming traffic, while I frantically pedalled, hoping he wouldn't check out my statement. I swung the bike around into the courtyard and propped the bike up against the graffitied wall where some young girls were playing two-ball. I ran up the steps to attend my patient who was supposed to be in the last stages of labour and knocked urgently on the yellow door.

'My, luv, you're in a hurry.'

I relaxed once the front door was closed. The only labour that seventy-year-old Mrs Leeson was contemplating was her labour of love in putting the kettle on for a cup of tea for me.

'Don't tell me you've come up that one-way again. It's really risky, nurse, now that new copper's there. He's only a young bloke but he won't stand any nonsense. His wife is Nurse Caplin, at the outpatients at King's. She was telling me she was working at the hospital on nights and they was turning out old chipped enamel water jugs. Chucking 'em out, you know, in the bin. Nurse Caplin, seeing as it wasn't wanted, took one 'ome for a coffee pot. They had a right dust-up. 'er 'usband told her she was a thief. She said 'e kept on about it so much, she took it back and threw it in the bin again. That shows you what 'e's like.'

'It is so ridiculous to have to go all the way around the one-way system.'

'You be careful, duckie. You 'ave only just got back from one accident.'

'Who told you that?' I asked indignantly. 'It couldn't have been one of the nurses.'

'I read it in the local paper about a nurse knocked off 'er bike by a lorry driver.'

'I thought someone had spoken out of turn.'

'What, one of you girls? That'd be the day. I reckon you girls got zips, not lips.'

We had a very strict code of conduct with regard to confidentiality. We were not allowed to divulge any information about patients, nurses or our private life.

When I first started on the district Miss

Wright instructed me about confidentiality and professionalism. If I wanted to keep my private life private, I had to keep it zipped. She didn't quite use those words, but it meant the same thing.

When Miss Wright accompanied me on my rounds, I was amazed to hear Mr Bowman address her and speak to her in a personal way.

'Hallo, Trudie, how are you? What became of that young doctor you were courting?'

Miss Wright looked intensely uncomfortable, blushed and fiddled with her silver Queen's badge.

'Oh, Mr Bowman, that was years ago. He went to America.' She sounded flustered.

'And your auntie, is she still alive?'

'No, she died about a year after Clive took up his post in the States.'

'I thought you were supposed to be going with him?'

'It wasn't to be, Mr Bowman, so let's leave it at that,' she replied curtly.

I was shocked, especially after all the lectures she had given us on confidentiality, and here was Mr Bowman, a patient, discussing her private life.

After we left the house Miss Wright said, 'There you are, nurse. You have just been given a very good reason why you should *not* tell anyone your private business. How was I to know that years later, I would still be here, and that I would become the Superintendent. Let that be a salutary lesson to you.'

It was. I followed it to the letter and rigidly adhered to its principle.

Mrs Leeson had glaucoma and had regular visits for eye drops. At first she required four visits a day, then three. Now, since her last hospital appointment, it had been reduced to two.

This, I can tell you, was a relief, not only because of the improvement that had taken place but, as every community nurse would confirm, it was frustrating having to travel long distances to attend a patient frequently, only for a matter of a few seconds. Sarah and I often used to try to think of an invention so that the patient could self-medicate eye drops. We felt we could save the country thousands of pounds in nurses' time. (I believe there is a gadget now.)

Today Mrs Leeson was subdued. She had attended the eye clinic at Outpatients the previous day, so I asked her how she got on.

'Very good really. After eight years I can come off the eye drops altogether – the last visit will be on Sunday.'

'That's marvellous, you will be free to go out and about again. Always having to get back or be home must have been very restrictive for you,' I said.

As much as all the nurses were fond of

Mrs Leeson, I knew they would be relieved after all these years to be able to take her off the books.

'I'll miss you all, you have been like the family I never had,' she said, wiping a tear from her cheek.

'I'll miss my cup of tea and a chat,' I said.

'You will still come and see me, won't you?'

How often had a patient said this when they were coming off the books? How often I had said, like all my colleagues, 'Yes I'll try.' So few patients had come off the books and so many had come on. With the pressure of work, promises such as this were all too easy make – so difficult to keep.

All the nurses made a special effort to drop in for a social call over the first month. We told ourselves that we did not want to create a dependency. We wanted Mrs Leeson to pick up the pieces of her life and regain her independence.

In retrospect – what pieces? She had few hobbies and interests. The district nurses had entered her home four times a day for eight years. We had entered her life. We *were* her life.

With all our best intentions, it didn't happen. We did not keep up the contact that we should have done, or put something else in its place. Many nurses were probably cheering that at last we had rid ourselves of this endless round of eye drops. Imagine four visits a day. What was there to talk about that we hadn't already discussed? The inconvenience of travelling the distance. The difficulty trying to fit in all four visits. With this line of thought it is easy to relieve one's conscience.

To Mrs Leeson we had managed it for eight years, so surely an occasional visit from one of us was not too much to ask, to show we still cared?

Six months later, Mrs Leeson was dead. She had taken her own life. Overnight when the visits stopped, she had lost her entire family. We had made a promise. She felt we had rejected her.

Mrs Duff was on my list and she required some abdominal sutures to be removed. When she opened the door we immediately recognised each other. Mrs Duff had been admitted to my ward four years ago as an attempted suicide. The police were waiting at her bedside for a statement. It was still an illegal act to try to take one's own life.

Thinking back, I remembered how Mrs Duff had called out for her daughter. Her daughter was ten years old. A callous nurse replied, 'You didn't think about your daughter when you wanted to end it all. Perhaps if you hadn't been so selfish and thought of her, you wouldn't have had to have your stomach pumped out.'

Her remarks were cruel and, although she was senior to me, I told her so.

I went into Mrs Duff's bedroom and started to remove her stitches.

'I remember you challenged that staff nurse... I had found out that my husband was having an affair with his secretary and he left me. I panicked. I didn't know what I was doing, I was in a state of shock. I walked the streets late at night. I must have picked up the bottle of pills before I left home. I know I went into a pub and asked for a pint of beer, then I took it outside the pub and swallowed the pills down. At the time I tried to end my life, I was so shocked and dazed, *I didn't even know I had a daughter.* I lost sight of everything. I not only tried to destroy myself but my family as well.'

'A lot of us are guilty of losing sight of the important things in life and we don't always get our priorities right,' I said. I was still raw from the death of Mrs Leeson.

I was not looking forward to my next visit. Mrs Rogers was always warm and friendly but her husband could be hostile and morose. The most he could offer for a greeting would be a sulky grunt. He wouldn't look up from his racing paper to acknowledge me in any way. His head always seemed to be immersed in the *Sporting Life*.

I had come to give Mrs Rogers her weekly

injection. I placed an old newspaper on the table. Mrs Rogers had dutifully laid out the equipment: a screw-top jam jar full of surgical spirit with a glass syringe and a smaller jar of needles also soaking in spirit. I took out my bottle of sterile water to rinse the equipment. There should have been a pair of forceps with the syringe but it was missing.

I washed my hands and plunged my fingers into the jam jar. There was too much spirit in the jar and it trickled over the top of the jar and soaked the newspaper. The injection over, I asked Mrs Rogers if she could tidy up the equipment.

'Certainly, no problem, nurse. You get along I know you are busy.'

I was washing my hands, getting ready to leave, when Mr Rogers got out of his chair and examined the table where the spirit had been spilt.

'Here you, you had better tell your boss I'm reporting you for damaging a very valuable table.'

At first I thought he was joking and I smiled at him. The Rogers had very few possessions. The table was already a mass of white heat stains where it had been used as an ironing table.

'Take no notice of him, dear, he doesn't know what he's saying,' said Mrs Rogers.

'You can shut up, woman. I know exactly what I'm saying.'

I apologised for any damage that I had caused and said I would report the accident to the office.

'Now this is what I want you to do, nurse,' said Miss Wright. 'You go back there this afternoon and you tell Mr Rogers that I was extremely angry with you and that I have said you will have the money deducted from your salary to pay for the damage.'

I looked at her in astonishment.

'It's all right, don't look so worried, I won't be deducting any money from your salary.'

I returned to the house and informed Mr Rogers that the Superintendent had said that every penny of his claim would be taken out of my wages.

His wife was upset. 'Henry, you can't let that happen to my nurse, it's unkind. It was an accident. She didn't do it deliberately. Besides, you know that table wasn't much cop.'

Reluctantly he agreed. 'Go on clear off,' he said. 'I'll let it drop this time.'

I reported back to the office as requested and told Miss Wright the outcome.

'Mm ... it works every time,' she said with a satisfied grin.

Chapter Twenty-two

'I've just come back from seeing Mr Kuznetzov,' said Sarah as she tossed her coat on the peg in the hall.

'How's his wife?' She had recently suffered a severe stroke.

'Oh, it's sad, Mik, they can't communicate. Her speech is coming back but she can only speak Russian. It wouldn't be so bad if her husband could understand her, but he's from a different region and he can only make out the odd word. It's frustrating for everyone. His son has written him. He reckons he can get his mother into a beautiful nursing home much better than here. No charge. Free. He showed me some photographs of his son's home. Looks wonderful, kid. A huge house overlooking a lake and mountains in the background. I think Mr Kuznetzov said that was just his holiday home. Mik, does that make sense?'

'Not to me it doesn't. I didn't think it was like that over there. I thought Jews were treated badly. His son seems to have everything. Don't you think that's odd? He's trying to persuade him to go and live in Russia,' I said.

We sat at the table playing our butter-soaked corn on the cobs like harmonicas. With Vernon away for three weeks in Trinidad and Roy away on a course, we were beginning to enjoy some time to ourselves without the rush to prepare special meals or get dressed up.

'We can be a couple of slobs for a bit,' said Sarah, 'and get some jobs done.'

'Slobs, you speak for yourself,' I said.

'What do you mean?' asked Sarah.

'What is it you say when it's your turn to clean? *It only take me half an hour to go through the house, when Mik's done it. Only to flick a duster and push the sweeper.*'

Sarah's mouth dropped open. 'Who told you that? Do you think after all this time I would...?'

'Skive like that? Yes. What did you say to me about dreaming?...*Wouldn't think anything bad about me, or you'll dream about it.*'

'You dreamed it?'

'Uh uh.'

'Wow! that's fantastic. Mik, it's true all of it,' she confessed.

'Yes I know,' I said.

Sarah began to laugh. 'I got away with it for two years, girl. You can't blame me. You always put on too much polish, enough for two weeks. I was economising with electricity and polish.'

I was economical with the truth. I had not

heard the conversation she had with her sister in my sleep but on the telephone. I didn't like to disillusion her, Sarah was such a great believer in dreams.

'Girl, I've been wanting to make myself a decent jacket for the winter, I've got the material. As soon as I fetch it out to start cutting, the phone rings and it's Vern coming over for the evening or one of the girls calling in to see if I've finished their garments. I don't get a chance to make anything for myself. Tonight girl, to hell with everyone I say, I'm looking after number one. I feel guilty, it's three weeks since I promised to finish Miss Harris's dress. It's for her friend's wedding next month. She's worried. She say she have many business functions before the wedding, she will need several alterations. I dread her come down and ask for it.'

'How far have you got?'

'Mik, don't ask, not a cut made, not a cotton threaded.'

'You mean you haven't even star–'

'Shh. Don't even think it, kid. She will be downstairs and catch me out.'

'But you've had the material for ages.'

'I know, I *know*, I keep *meaning* to. It put me off when she say it will need lots of alterations. Why don't I wait for her to balloon out on dinners and *then* get started?'

'Sarah, quick, get the material out, I can hear a muffled sound. It could be, it could be ... yes it is ... it's Miss Harris coming now to see the finished dress,' I teased.

'Oh it's not funny, I'm not giving you a joke.'

'Seriously though, I *can* hear something. It's coming from the hallway.' I peered around the door into the hall. 'Sarah, are you expecting anything? I think someone's left a big parcel in the doorway. I can see it through the glass.'

I sauntered down the passageway, to open the door and thought I heard a groan. I opened the door. A blood-stained bundle fell into the hall. I recognised the face and let out a shout.

'Sarah, quick. It's Beverley. She's bleeding like crazy.'

Blood pumped relentlessly, drenching her skirt and stockings. Her face was like alabaster. We carried her to the bedroom. Sarah grabbed towels from the clothes horse and threw them on the bed.

'What is she doing here? I'll get an ambulance,' I said, walking towards the telephone.

'No, not yet,' said Sarah. 'Wait, let me look at her first.'

Sarah carefully examined her abdomen and Bev let out an agonised wail.

'Mik,' she said in a hushed tone, 'she's had an abortion – it look like that woman Nora from Camberwell.'

Beverley opened her eyes and looked at her surroundings. She seemed relieved when she recognised us.

'I'm really sorry, Sarah – I had nowhere else to go. I thought I'd be OK but I couldn't go back to the nurses' home. I must have fainted.'

'Ssh, it's OK, Bev. Don't worry, you are safe with us,' said Sarah.

Young people today have enormous burdens placed on them with regard to drink drugs and sex. We had different types of pressures. Sex was to be avoided at all costs; reliable contraception was not available. As I have already said, having a baby outside marriage held an enormous stigma. It forced young people to seek out back-street abortionists and herbalists in an attempt to rid themselves of unwanted pregnancies. Illegal abortions would often take place on a Friday evening, to give the girl a chance to recover over the week-end. Hopefully she would be fit to return to work on the Monday. No questions were asked, as a safeguard for the abortionist.

Some would try to induce themselves by taking a variety of herbal medicines. Or worse, resort to practical methods. The insertion of a knitting needle was commonplace. The potential danger of perforating the uterus was ignored in an overwhelming despair to get rid of the baby. Many women died of haemorrhage and septicaemia. Any method used was considered illegal. Women would sometimes tumble downstairs. This could then appear to be an accident and would seem a 'safer' option.

The contraceptive pill was not readily available at this time and women were still wary and worried about side effects. When it did become available, at first it was only given to married women. Once the pill became available to all women, the women were able to take control of their own bodies and decide how many children they wanted or could afford. This freedom for women was unprecedented.

'Sarah, don't you think we had better get a doctor?' I was beginning to panic at the amount of blood Bev had lost. Sarah ignored me.

'Does your own GP know you are pregnant?' Sarah asked.

'Yes, he said there was nothing he could do. I was healthy and I would have to go through with it.'

'Mik, give me a hand with the bed,' said Sarah.

Between us we lifted the foot of the bed and rested it on two bedroom chairs.

'How *could* I go through with it?' sniffed Bev, starting to cry.

'What happen about Martin, the Surgical Registrar? I thought you were getting married in March,' said Sarah.

'We were, but he broke off the engagement when I told him I was pregnant. I thought he might change his mind. He told me to get rid of it. He said he no longer loved me. We were not *intellectually compatible*, he said.' She started to cry. 'He's with that French registrar that joined Mr Raymond's firm last year.'

Sarah palpated Bev's abdomen again. This time the pain had eased and the bleeding stopped.

'Bev, you were lucky,' said Sarah. 'You could perforate your uterus.'

'I-I ... know,' sobbed Bev.

'I'm going to *have* to get a doctor to you. Mik, what about your GP? He seem an understanding man. Do you think he come to Beverley? If he give her ergometrine to contract the uterus and antibiotics for infection, we could try and keep Bev at home here for a few days.'

'I could try and see if he would come out. What about Miss Wright, what will we tell her?'

'You say she taken ill with gastric flu,' said Sarah. 'Maybe your doctor put *abdominal pain* on her certificate.'

I went upstairs in trepidation, to make the phone call. Doctor Swartz sounded concerned and arrived promptly.

'You silly girl, what have you been doing to yourself?' he said kindly. He examined her. 'Oh no, this looks like Nora's handiwork,' he said.

Sarah nodded in agreement.

He pulled down Bev's lower eyelids and drew breath sharply. 'Beverley, you know I should send you to hospital.'

Bev shook her head and looked at him, her eyes pleading.

'I'll give you an injection to stop the bleeding and another for infection. You will need something now for pain. What I give you for pain should make you sleep.'

'Thank you, doctor,' said Bev weakly.

Dr Swartz bent over and whispered something in Bev's ear and she nodded.

'Beverley, you are very lucky to have as your friends a midwife and a district nurse to care for you. I will come back tomorrow to see you.'

He took us to one side. 'Keep checking on her. Any further bleeding, you ring me straight away. I've left something for pain. If you need anything, you must contact me. I'll help you this once.'

'Thank you, doctor,' said Sarah.

'We'll look after her,' I said, shaking his hand.

As Sarah escorted him to the door, he said, 'Please be careful.'

We knew what he meant.

'I'm sorry to give you all this trouble,' said Bev.

'That's OK,' said Sarah. 'It's no problem.' She sighed and looked upwards showing the whites of her eyes.

No problem ... it was one hell of a problem and something we had to keep strictly to ourselves. We looked in on Bev before going to bed and I made up a makeshift bed on the sofa.

A hollow scream awoke me. We both rushed in to Beverley, who was sobbing and bathed in perspiration.

'Are you all right?' I asked.

'I dreamed I was going through it all over again.'

Her face was translucent and her body shaking. A light suddenly appeared on the stairs – it was Miss Harris.

'What's going on down there? It's nearly midnight.' She was standing on the landing in her dressing gown.

'We have a friend staying with us, I think she have a nightmare,' said Sarah.

'Sounded more like a woman in labour to me,' remarked Miss Harris. 'By the way, Sarah, I keep meaning to ask you, have you finished my dress yet?'

Sarah glanced across at me, and grimaced. 'Just another couple of days and it will be finished, Miss Harris.'

'Splendid, splendid. I must get some sleep, my friend is coming tomorrow from Canada to stay two weeks.' She disappeared to her room.

'That's all I need,' Sarah sighed.

I started to mumble a song to myself, *'There may be trouble ahead but while there's—'*

'OK, OK. I know I'll have to *face the music*, if I don't do her dress,' said Sarah.

I popped my head around the door of the bedroom.

'Are you all right? Is there anything I can get you?' I asked Bev.

She began to get upset again. 'Oh Monika, I can't get it out of my head, you wouldn't believe how awful it was today.'

I sat on the end of the bed and held her hand as she spoke of her harrowing experience.

'The first thing she wanted was the money. She snatched it and counted it. The place was filthy. I was about to run out when she came back and gave me a dirty nightdress to put on. *Come on, hurry up, put it on.* Then I had to step up on to a wooden platform with a doctor's type of couch on it.

'Come on, get a move on let's get on with it. Open your legs. I can't do it with your toes wrapped around the nightdress. Hurry up, I haven't got all bleeding day. You didn't get the chavi with your legs crossed. You know how it got there, the bloody thing has to come out the same

254

way it went in.

'She was so crude, so disgusting, not a bit sympathetic. *You forget, I'm doing you a big favour. I could go to prison for you.* She was horrible. Then she took hold of this long jagged metal instrument and thrust it inside me. I thought I was going to die. It felt like a dozen razor blades being forced in me. When I screamed she screeched at me, *Shut up, shut up, you little slut. You got yourself into this mess and then you want me to get you out of it.*

'I thought it was all over, then she drew something into a syringe. I felt the cold nozzle. Then I could smell tar, I'm sure it was Lysol. I remember thinking she's surely not going to give me that without diluting it? You know how corrosive that stuff is. You only have to get a small drop on you and you can get a burn.'

I let her talk on without interruption for what seemed like hours. I felt she needed to unburden herself.

'Oh God, that was worse, like a poker from a furnace. I was sick everywhere. I think I fainted. *Get up. Get up,* she shrieked, *I haven't got all day. Do you think you are the only one?*

'I didn't know how I was going to stand, let alone walk. I still don't know how I got my clothes back on. Later I remember holding on to the outside wall. I asked her if I could have a taxi? *What, and have the taxi driver get the fuzz on me,* she bawled.

255

'She even threatened to send some bully boys after me if I dared tell anyone where I'd been. A neighbour came out of her front door. I suppose she had seen it all before. I don't remember what happened next. The lady must have got me a taxi, because the next thing I knew, a man's voice said, *Where to, love?*

'I didn't know where to go. I just prayed that you would be in.'

I sponged her face with some cool water. 'It's all over now, Bev. In a few days you will feel fine.' I hoped she would. She looked terrible, she had a temperature and was sweating profusely.

We looked after Bev as best we could. We had to go to work during the day, but we worked out a rota between us and came home to check on her.

Dr Swartz was marvellous; he called in every day and gave her antibiotics. He was very understanding and compassionate.

'Do you know, Beverley, you are the same age as my daughter. I would hate to think that if my daughter made a mistake, she would go to the same lengths as you did to get rid of a baby. It's barbaric, and it's time the law was changed and the back-street abortionist put out of business.'

It was to take another five years before that would happen. The Abortion Law Reform Association had already been set up in 1936 to campaign for legal abortions in Britain in an effort to halt the number of deaths of women from back-street abortionists. It was common knowledge that they were operating unscrupulously and in unhygienic conditions. The reform association was also set up to prevent women from trying self-induced abortions with crude methods. There were campaigns and lobbying, and eventually, through the association's efforts, in 1967 the Abortion Act was passed. This was a tremendous step forward.

After a week, Beverley spoke of going back to the nurses' home. Dr Swartz wouldn't hear of it. He arranged for her to go into a private convalescent home at Broadstairs in Kent. As far as I know, her secret was safe. But she struggled to overcome her guilt. Dr Swartz couldn't believe her former boyfriend, a doctor, could have been so heartless to such a lovely girl.

Chapter Twenty-three

Mr Kuznetzov had emptied his display cabinet. All his medals were spread out on the table. He stroked his thinning white beard and stared at them as though mesmerised.

'I'm thinking of selling them, I need to see

my son in the Soviet Union. He has written to me that there are some lovely old people's homes near him. It makes sense for us to move there, he is the only family we have left.'

'It won't be the same without you,' I said. 'We will miss you.'

'That is kind of you. I haven't made up my mind yet, but I thought if I sold these,' he pointed to his medals, 'I could take the trip and see for myself. The doctor said that Tasha could go into St Francis Hospital for a fortnight, while I make the journey and make up my mind.'

'What does your son do in Russia?'

'He is a doctor in the army. He had a real struggle to become accepted as a doctor. He went into the army and tried hard to get promotion, but couldn't get any further than junior doctor rank.'

'Why was that?' I asked.

'Simple, he is a Jew. Suddenly, everything changed overnight. God gave my son a golden opportunity. Everything was made possible, through Nikita Khrushchev.'

'How was that?'

'The Premier of the Soviet Union, Nikita Khrushchev, happened to be visiting the army camp. He suddenly collapsed. He was taken critically ill with a heart attack. My son rushed to him and gave him emergency treatment. It was looking very bad but my son would not give up. Against all odds, he saved his life. For my son, his life changed completely. He was given the highest honours and awarded a special medal. From now on he could have anything he wanted, a large house in the country, promotion, anything.'

'That's wonderful. He has a higher rank now?'

'Oh yes, nurse, as a doctor, the highest. He says he can get us into some superb housing for the elderly, with nurses to look after Tasha. It is not very far from where he lives. Look, here's a photograph of his home – it's near the river and the forest. This is one of his other homes, the one he uses for his holidays.'

'You must be very proud of him.'

'Oh yes.'

'The photographs are beautiful,' I said, as I handed them back. 'The scenery is wonderful.'

Within a couple of weeks, Sarah called in to wish him well and to help me pack his wife's case, ready for her admission to hospital. Mr Kuznetzov had bought a new hat and overcoat for the trip and was very excited at the prospect of returning to his homeland.

On our way home, we ran into an old friend of ours, Pippa. We had done our general training together.

'How was your holiday, Pippa? Where did

you go?' I asked.

'Spain. It was lovely, but I ran out of money. I hadn't enough money to get to the airport or to get home from Heathrow.'

'What did you do?' asked Sarah.

'I had to go to the British Embassy to borrow some money.'

We looked in amazement at her. 'Pippa, only you could do that and get away with it,' I said.

'Anyone else would have found themselves clamped in irons and thrown in jail,' said Sarah, laughing. 'How are you getting on with midder?'

'I'm fed up with midwifery, I didn't realise it would be such a messy business. I think I'll get married,' she said calmly.

We looked again in astonishment at her.

'What! Marry, which one?' I asked.

'I have no idea yet,' she admitted.

There were at least three contenders. It was easy to see why; she was blonde and had a waif-like figure, similar to Audrey Hepburn's. She was also zany, witty and attractive, and had been engaged to them all in turn. She kept them dangling on a string, then she cast each one aside – you could say like a passing fiancé.

'Why so urgent to get married?' asked Sarah.

'When I looked at my passport in Spain, I realised I was beginning to really look like my passport photograph, so I thought I'd better get married while the men were still asking.' She tossed her shimmering hair from her face and began to laugh. 'I think I will marry–' She paused for a few seconds. 'Yes, I think I will marry Ken, he's *always* asking me.'

We stood open-mouthed, unable to believe what we had just heard. This was hardly going to be a marriage made in heaven.

'You must let me have your address, and I'll send you an invitation.'

We couldn't believe how casually she had regarded matrimony.

'Talk about spur of the moment,' I said.

'I think she jealous of her younger sister that marry last year,' said Sarah.

'Could be. If so, she's crazy.'

As we prepared our meal I thought about Mr Kuznetzov.

'I wonder how he's getting on.'

'I can see why that man get everything now. Just imagine what would happen if he let Khrushchev die,' said Sarah.

'Oh yes, that would have been terrible. His father wouldn't be going to stay at a luxury villa by the lake. He'd be trekking his way to the salt mines to visit him.'

We hadn't long to wait to find out. Within two weeks Mr Kuznetzov was back home.

'How did it go?' I asked.

'Oh nurse, the homes my son showed me were beautiful, but I couldn't go back now,' he said. 'It was lovely to see my son, his wife and my grandson, but no, I couldn't go back. In fact I don't know how he can live like it,' he said sadly.

'Like what?'

'When I arrived my head was buzzing with questions. I just didn't think, I asked him where the synagogue was and about the rumours of people being locked up in prison for their religion. I told him I had read in England about a woman who had been handing out bookmarks with the words from the Psalms of David. She was put in prison. Was it true, I asked him.'

'Yes, I read that. What did he say?'

'That's it, *he wouldn't say*, he *couldn't* say anything. When we were at the airport I didn't know what I was doing was wrong. He tried to stop me speaking. He seemed very nervous. What is the matter, son, I kept asking him. *I'll tell you later Papa*, he said.

'Later he took me to the edge of the forest. Something is very wrong here, I can't speak to you, I said. *Papa – everywhere is bugged, you can't talk religion or politics in Russia now.*

'Everywhere is bugged, son? I couldn't believe it. *Yes, even the bedrooms*, he said. *We are safe here to speak. If you want to talk of such things you must go to the woods.*

'This is terrible, I don't know how you are

able to live like this. *Papa I know all the places that are bugged so I watch what I say, it's quite easy – I'm used to it. We know not to talk politics. As for religion, it is just for a few old people. Young people don't bother with it now.*

'Don't bother with it? Son, you have all the trappings of wealth but you are not rich, you are poor. The peasants living out here are happier than you. They have more freedom than you. They can speak freely to each other where they live, without fear. You think you have everything – you have nothing. What you think you were given, you have paid dearly for. In exchange, you have given them your soul.'

'I hugged and kissed him, and told him I can't come back to live. I have tasted freedom in England too long. We both cried. We knew that we would probably never see each other again.'

'I am really sorry,' I said, putting my arm around his shoulder.

'Don't be, nurse. It taught me a lesson going back. We don't appreciate what we have until we have lost it. Here we take freedom for granted. We have happiness but we don't recognise it until it is too late or over. Have you ever said, I am happy now, at this exact moment?'

I shook my head. 'No I haven't.'

'Usually we say it when we look back in time, yes?'

I nodded.

'When I got my degree, that was my happiest moment. Or when I met my wife was the happiest time of my life. Some people think all they need to do to be happy is to win the football pools. Would that be real happiness? No, soon there would be arguments. What do we do with the money?'

'Yes, I suppose that's true,' I said.

'Believe me, nurse, money does not bring happiness. There are more arguments over money than anything else. People either have too much or too little. Going back to Russia I learned a big lesson. Over there, I would never feel free from fear, and that I should appreciate that freedom is the most precious gift of all. Sadly, for a lot of people they don't get to realise this until they have lost it. I had a second chance to come back here and embrace it once again.'

As I rode off to my next patient I thought on what Mr Kuznetzov had said about freedom and happiness. Tommy Steele's 'Handful of Songs' echoed in my ears; *Happiness – no more – no less*. I hummed the tune as I cycled.

It must have been a couple of weeks after Mr Kuznetzov returned when I met Pippa outside the post office.

Her marriage to Ken had been by special licence, but unfortunately neither of us could

264

get there as we were both working. When I met her she had only been married three weeks.

'How's married life?' I asked.

'*Comme ci, comme ça.* It's not going all that well.'

'What do you mean?'

'It's not all that it's cracked up to be,' she said. 'Don't let's talk about that. I've got some fabulous news – I met the most smashing man in the park yesterday.'

'What! Didn't you tell him you were married?'

'He noticed my wedding ring.'

'Considering it's about two inches wide, I'm not surprised that he noticed it,' I said. 'What did you tell him?'

'I told him I just wore the ring to keep the wolves away,' she said, unperturbed. 'You must come over and see me sometime. Bring Sarah,'

'Mm. I'll try.'

Somehow, I didn't think I would be able to persuade Sarah. She was preoccupied and seemed to be spending a lot of time in the upstairs flat, talking to Miss Harris's Canadian friend.

Chapter Twenty-four

'Pippa telephoned when you were out,' said Sarah.

'Did she say what she wanted?'

'For you to go over, I think. They're living in Hampstead – Ken's got his dental practice there.'

I telephoned her.

'Why don't you and Sarah come over and see us? Stay over if you like.'

'That would be great,' I said. 'We could talk about old times.'

As I spoke, Sarah shook her head.

'Sarah's pretty busy at the moment, but I'll come over.'

'This is a lovely flat you have here, Pippa, it's so spacious.'

'Ken has some rooms above, for his reception and surgery. This was his friend's flat, he went back to Australia. I'm only sorry that I have to work on Saturday morning, but you are welcome to come with me if you want to.'

'Yes, I'd like to.'

Pippa was a community midwife in a very smart area of London. The type of homes that she visited would doubtless bear little resemblance to my working patch. Mary Quant and mini skirts had not yet appeared on the scene. Most of the women were wearing dresses and skirts with a tiered underskirt giving a puffball appearance. Hampstead, however, had gone for the maxi. Long skirts and coats dusted the pavements.

Pippa had the oddest dress sense. She constantly wore an incredibly scruffy coat that flopped over her feet. When she first acquired it, it had been a light beige trench coat, now it looked as though it had served its time in the trenches. It was a mottled, muddy-grey colour, the sort of item that even the Red Cross would have put in the bin, having thought it unsuitable for a flood victim.

Pippa was indifferent to her offbeat appearance. For her, of paramount importance was that this tatty garment still had intact its Harrods label.

'Do you know, darling,' she said to me when I arrived, 'I ordered a delightful escritoire from Harrods and the driver had the audacity to park his van halfway down Haverlock Hill. How ridiculous! How are one's neighbours supposed to know who had ordered it?

'Yet when Ken bought a chaise longue from a dubious antique shop, I could not get rid of the delivery man. He made sure he parked right outside the flat. Would you believe, he had brought it on a horse and cart. The neighbours knew all about *that*. I refused to give the man a tip and he spent half the morning feeding his horse and guzzling bottles of beer outside. Evelyn's gardener, a tomato grower, enjoyed himself and kept the neighbours amused. He fed the horse apples, then ran over later with a bucket and shovel.'

We set off to do the visits at eight in the morning. The streets were deserted, the residents did not start to stir until about midday. At midnight the streets would be teeming with people, coming from pubs and coffee bars, linking arms and walking along laughing and talking, as though it were the middle of the afternoon.

The first visit of the morning was at the home of a show business personality. The new mum had been a choreographer to the stars. She had taught several comedians and actors whenever their performances required dance routines.

We walked into the nursery. It was like entering the enchanted fairy grotto at Christmas. The baby, bedecked in lace, peered through a gossamer-swathed crib.

Yvette lived with her parents. They had their own successful industrial business. In the drawing room there were two pianos, one a white grand, the other a mahogany upright.

Both were easily accommodated in this palatial room. It was easily large enough to double up as a dance studio when necessary.

'Would you like to see my new Tudor room?' enquired the grandmother.

'I'd love to,' I said.

As we walked towards the dark panelled room I endeavoured to make conversation.

'You must be delighted, she's beautiful,' I said, referring to the baby.

'Illegitimate, you know,' she said.

With Yvette in show business when the unconventional was the norm, I tried to smooth things over.

'I'm sure no one takes any notice, these days,' I said.

'Some of my friends can be very pernickety about it. I don't care what they think, I think it's lovely.' She stroked the arm of one of the chairs. 'I know it is not legitimate Tudor, it is only repro, but you must admit it is very clever how they make the arms of the chairs look so old and worn.'

For what could have been an enormous boot in the mouth job, I heaved a sigh of relief. I happily interjected with the usual pleasing remarks – wonderful, lovely, fascinating – as I admired the new Tudor room.

Pippa had finished her visit to the mother and baby and was sitting on the sofa. A tray of coffee on the table awaited us. As we relaxed, a huge St Bernard lolloped across

269

the room.

'I hope Hector, hasn't been in the pond again. Be careful, he loves the water. Do you know, Diana Dors' (Granny dropped more names than Brian Rix used to drop trousers) 'was sitting where you are, when the dog hurtled in, straight from the pond. He leaped up on Diana's lap. She was soaked and smothered in mud. Water dripped everywhere. But she is a real trouper, she didn't mind a bit, she could see how funny it was.'

'That's strange, I had always imagined her to be the feisty type,' I said.

'Oh, no, not at all, not a bit.'

We drove off past the pond on our way out.

'Can you believe what we just heard? Are we talking about the same Diana Dors that played Ruth Ellis in *Yield to the Night*? The woman that was friendly with the notorious Kray family?'

Pippa shook her head. 'If a soaking wet dog the size of a heifer landed on me, I can assure you I would not mince my words. Like a trouper? *Swore* like one, more like it.'

It was only a few weeks after my visit to Hampstead that Pippa rang me again. She sounded upset.

'Can you come over and see me? Ken and I are splitting up. We had a bit of a row.' She started to cry. This was out of character; she was usually the stiff upper lip sort.

I felt sorry for her, beneath her tough exterior she was a softy really. Too soft when it came to the patients, especially when she was a student. When we worked together, I was shocked to discover a patient had gone missing out of an oxygen tent. He was obviously not fit enough to get out and walk.

'I can't use the bedpan in bed, nurse. Can't you take me to the proper toilet?'

'Come on then,' said Pippa, 'I'll get you a wheelchair and take you down there.'

The fact that he was turning purple and gasping for air didn't seem to concern her.

Another time when she was taking a meal to a patient, it was, 'Diabetic? What a shame. I'm sure you could have a tiny piece of cake, quick, while no one is looking.'

If Pippa and Ken had a row, it could be a humdinger.

I walked right into the middle of 'a domestic' – they were shouting at each other and throwing things.

'I think I'd better come back another day,' I said, as Pippa tossed another bundle of clothes from the wardrobe out of the window.

By now clothes were strewn all the way up the garden path. Pyjama bottoms were waving from trees like flags on students' rag week. She was none too bothered about the neighbours this time.

After a short time I decided to leave and made my way back to the station. I looked back from the top of the road. Y-fronts of all colours could be seen flapping from the trees.

Chapter Twenty-five

When I got back from Hampstead, Sarah was waiting up for me. She looked anxious. It soon became apparent why. Sarah had been spending a lot of time with Miss Harris's Canadian friend and was intent on emigrating to Canada.

She was animated as she described Calgary, where she was hoping to go. She was so excited, yet inevitably her happiness was tinged with sadness. We knew this would be the end of an era. We hugged each other. What could I say except, 'I am very pleased for you and I hope it works out all right for you both.'

'Mik, Vern isn't coming with me.'

'What do you mean? I thought you were crazy about each other?'

'He hasn't got sufficient qualifications.'

'Yes, but he can get them.'

'The problem is, girl, he don't want to trouble himself.'

'Once he realises you're so keen to go, I'm sure he will do something about it.'

Soon after Sarah broke the news. Miss Hams stopped me.

'Sarah's hoping to go to Calgary, you know.'

'Yes, she mentioned Calgary to me.'

'I don't like to disappoint her, she was so enthusiastic about going to the same place as my friend.'

'What's wrong, why can't she go there?'

'I've told her to apply, but she won't get in there.'

'Why not?'

'My friend said that they don't take black people in Calgary.'

'But that's stupid, she's set her heart on that area, and she has triple qualifications. She's a Registered Nurse, midwife and Queen's Nurse,' I said in disbelief.

'Yes, I know, dear, I told my friend that. She said it won't make any difference. They won't accept black people in that area. They will send her to some far-flung place in Canada.'

There wasn't anything I could say, only hope for Sarah's sake that Miss Harris would be proved wrong. I never mentioned our conversation to Sarah.

Vernon had become moody ever since he heard about Canada.

'Why you want to go there, girl? I thought you were happy here.'

'I think there will be better opportunities there for us.'

'You mean for you, I won't be able to get work there, you already told me that.'

'Not without some qualifications, they don't recognise the ones you got in Trinidad.'

'Man, you Miss High and Mighty. You have it made, you got yours.'

'I know, Vern. How long have I been telling you get qualified?'

'You had this all planned. That why you keep saying go to night school, go to night school. I got a question for you. S'pose I don't go to night school?'

'Vern, my mind is made up. If you love me – you will follow me.'

'Huh, that easy to say, man. I ain't going to find it easy to study when you not here.'

'Sometimes, Vernon, when things are too easy, they are not worth having. If you think I am worth it, you will try to join me later. If you work hard now, the time won't be too long.'

'It all sounds great for you. Not for me. I can't start studying now, can I, Mik?'

'Of course you can, Vernon. You will just have to set your mind to it,' I said.

Sarah let out a big sigh, looked at me and shook her head in exasperation. Vernon plonked himself down on the sofa. He looked sullen. As Sarah passed my chair she whispered, 'Just ignore him, he come round, he just in a moody.'

I put the record player on and put on the flip side of the record that Vernon had bought for the party. There was a cheerful little calypso on the back, which I thought might lighten up the atmosphere. It mentioned the jobs that parents do for their children.

I say remember who
Who used to wash your clothes for you
Who used to find your supper
Who used to hug and kiss you
Don't forget 'twas your mother and father

'There you are, Vern, *remember who wash your clothes, who find your supper* – I'm more like your mother,' said Sarah. 'Unless you get studying, you soon *have* to find your own supper and take yourself down that laundrette.'

Vernon looked up and started to grin. 'OK, you win, Sal. I'll call in the college tomorrow.'

Sarah went over to him and kissed him, a long passionate kiss. 'You'd miss me, you know you would.'

'I'd miss your cooking more,' he said with a grin.

Sarah began a mock fight with him. He pulled her on to the sofa with a laugh. I left the room with Sarah and Vernon in a romantic clinch, and went in the kitchen to get the supper.

My life was richer for having known Sarah and Vernon. I had learned that people, whatever their colour, religion or culture, all want the same things. We all want a good job. We want a home and a good education for our children. We want to feel safe and secure. We want to feel needed, loved and respected.

As for Sarah and me, everything would change from now on. Little did I know Miss Harris's friend from Canada would turn our lives upside down.

I would miss Sarah – not just the sharing of a home and traditional dishes. It was much more than that. We had shared our problems, our troubles, our hopes and aspirations for the future. Now, once again, we were both at the crossroads.

Chapter Twenty-six

Bob Mitchell was not cheerful. Neither was he pleasant. He was not a man to have a joke with. Bob Mitchell was a moaner. If it wasn't the weather it was his food, or his wife, but, most of all, he moaned about being unable to walk properly. He had suffered a stroke some seven years previously.

For seven years everyone had suffered Bob. He was manipulative and moody, his one

276

pleasure in life was to watch others dance attendance on him. A wry smile would appear on his face when he eventually got his own way.

Jane had been a primary school teacher. She was used to dealing with children demanding her attention. When she left the school to devote her life to her husband she thought it would be simple; after all, she just had the one pupil to deal with.

'What ever is that low moving cloud?' said Sarah as we set off for our afternoon visits. I was supposed to be visiting Bob Mitchell and he could be nasty if I was late.

'I've no idea, I've never seen anything like it.' As I spoke, the sun disappeared under the twisting, turbulent blanket. We had run into a plague of flying ants. Huge, brown, bat-like insects that had swirled through London one summer afternoon.

Motorists had screeched to a halt as their windscreens were obliterated with a crawling brown canopy. Windscreen wipers seized up as the flying army clung to them in their attempt to choke the city.

People in the street were held in the grip of a brown fog, except that this was a legion of living, creeping creatures. One minute the sound of heavy vehicles clanking through the town, cars and taxis hooting and the shrill ringing of bells on bikes; the next silence, all vehicles having been brought to a halt. A deathlike hush stilled the London traffic for several hours during the invasion of these strange flying insects.

If motorists were troubled, you can just imagine what it was like cycling through them. At least motorists were protected and in the safety of the car even if they could not continue with their journey. The winged creatures flew in our eyes, crawled in our ears and down our necks. Worst of all, they battled their way into our mouths and we were constantly spitting them out.

We had to stop. There was no way we could fight them. Sarah clawed at her head as they imbedded themselves in her thick hair. At one point we had to be rescued by the police, when they found us marooned on a grassy bank in the middle of a roundabout. We had both become disorientated. Then, like an apocalypse, it passed over the area and the traffic started to move again.

As I feared, I arrived late at Mr Mitchell's. His wife was very understanding and had been concerned, but Bob Mitchell started moaning, 'Don't you come bringing any bloody ants in here. I've got enough to put up with without you adding to it.'

'Bob dear, don't go on at the nurse, it's not her fault. Don't take any notice of him, nurse, he's in a bad mood today.'

Bad mood, that was a joke, he was always in a bad mood. I felt sorry for his wife. She had such patience with him but I noticed she had lost weight and was looking very tired.

'Oh, I'm fine, nurse, except for these headaches. I keep saying I must go to the doctor, but you know how it is with Bob. He takes up all my time.'

I tried to persuade her to see her GP but I wasn't convinced she would take my advice. Jane had not had a holiday or a break of any kind since her husband's stroke. Apart from a weekly visit for a bath, Jane did the rest of the care.

'I wouldn't put him in a home just so that I would have a break, that wouldn't be fair,' she said. 'Besides, he would never forgive me. Bob says if he went into a home it would kill him.' It was emotional blackmail.

I was surprised the following week to be greeted at the gate by his daughter.

'Mum died yesterday, she had a massive stroke and never recovered.'

I offered my condolences and asked where her father was.

'He's in a naval home. He had paid twopence a week when he was in the Navy, in the event that he might need looking after in his old age.'

A few weeks later I decided to go and see him. I had heard that the home was very modern with a bar and a bowling green in the grounds. I was really more interested in seeing the naval home than Bob.

Bob was *walking* in the grounds with one of the residents. He was walking unaided apart from one stick. He called out to me, 'Hello, nurse. Fancy seeing you.'

He was so cheerful I had to make sure it was the same person.

'Mr Mitchell?' I asked.

'Come and sit over here on this bench,' he said.

He was a changed man. Was it the all-male environment, being back with the lads? Whatever it was, I was stunned. This was a miracle. Later I asked the staff if I could look around the home.

Over each bed there was a shield that bore the name of the ship in which the sailor had served. There were two comfortable lounges. One was a quiet room, the other had a television and a bar. Leading off this room was the billiard room. If the men became bored strolling through the grounds, there was always the attractive park opposite. Bob told me he often took a walk in the park. 'In fact, most days I'm over there.'

One Sunday afternoon when Roy was home on leave, we happened to walk through the park. I could see the reason for Bob's sudden improved health and mobility and the reason for his interest in frequenting the park. Sitting on the bench was a smartly dressed lady in her mid-seventies and holding her hand was Bob.

I pulled at Roy's arm to steer him on a different route as I didn't want Bob to know I had seen him.

Six months later, I met his daughter in Jones and Higgins in Rye Lane, Peckham. She told me that her father had married and moved into a new bungalow. At seventy-five, I reckon he could have won an Oscar.

When we arrived back at the flat Sarah was busy in the kitchen. Vernon was coming over and she was preparing supper for the four of us. I put the kettle on for tea.

'I am making flitters,' said Sarah.

She had soaked the dried salt fish overnight and was gently flaking it into a bowl. In the batter she was tossing in some herbs and spices. Gradually she added the fish. Fat sizzled in the frying pan as spoonfuls of small pancakes were dropped in. A large pan full of peas and pink rice was warming through on the other hob. Golden brown flitters, peas and rice with green salad.

'Mm, I love the smell of the fish and spices. 'tis fit for a king,' I said.

'It is only simple food.'

'So you say, but I love it.'

'You love it because you don't have to cook it.'

'Could be. It is a lot of fiddling about soaking this and that. Then it's eaten in minutes.'

We still took it in turns to cook one week,

clean the next. And we still had Caribbean food one week and British the next, although I had noticed that rice or sweet potato had a habit of creeping into all meals regardless. I started to pour the tea.

'Tomorrow night, Roy suggested going out as a foursome for a meal. Are you off, Sarah?'

'Yes, I'm off in the evening. Where are we going?'

'He has left it to us to choose. Any ideas?'

'Not at the moment. I may think of somewhere suitable in the morning.'

As we got ready for work, we tried to think of an impressive restaurant. Sarah was brushing her teeth in the bathroom. As usual, I was darning a huge hole in my stocking.

'What about that smart restaurant we took Miss Harris to for her fortieth?' said Sarah.

'The Peacock?' I called out.

'Yes, that was really nice and the food gorgeous.'

Sarah appeared with a turban wrapped around her head, still clutching her toothbrush.

'Yes, it was a friendly place. We had that lovely buffet at lunchtime,' she said.

'Did we get a tube from the Elephant? It was at Westminster, wasn't it? It was very popular with businessmen,' I said.

'You won't be very popular, Mik. Don't forget your bike's in again with its chain off.'

'Oh dear, I'll have to run for the bus *again*,' I said as I grabbed my coat from the hall. The previous morning I was nowhere near the stop when I saw the bus hurtling down Dog Kennel Hill. I leapt out and without thinking stuck out my hand like a policeman directing traffic. To my astonishment it worked. The bus stopped.

'Where the bloody 'ell do you think you are, 'op-picking in the country? You can't stop London Transport just like that. Go on then ... 'op on.'

That was yesterday. Here I was again, with the red double-decker trundling down the hill and the bus stop another five hundred yards to go. I'd never make it. Just as I began to slacken my pace a familiar voice called out, 'Don't worry, nurse. I'll stop it for you.' It was Janet Simpson, the lady whose stitches I had removed. Janet made a positive move forward on to the zebra crossing, placing one foot firmly in position. The bus driver, seeing that she was about to cross and had already placed one foot on the zebra, had no choice, he had to stop. With a snarling and squealing of brakes the bus ground to a halt, inches from the crossing.

'Go on, nurse, get on the bus. I'll hold it back for you,' shouted Janet, deliberately strolling across the road like an action replay.

'Bugger me, I've seen it all now. If you

can't stop it yourself, you get some other poor bugger to do it for you,' said the irate bus driver.

When I got on the bus, the passengers were laughing and some tutting at the audacity.

'I don't know how you had the cheek to do it *again*,' said Sarah, laughing.

'I've got my bike back now, thank goodness.'

'Mik, before you start your *I haven't got a rag to wear* cry, I've finished your black and rust outfit, so you could wear that tonight.'

'Thanks, Sarah, that's wonderful.'

When we arrived at the restaurant there seemed a different atmosphere.

'I don't remember all these alcoves and mirrors, do you, Sarah?'

'It certainly looks different at night.'

The clientele had changed. Encircled in coils of wormlike smoke sat a woman of fifty, with bottle-blonde ringlets, crossed-legged on a bar stool, flashing her white leather thigh boots and welded into a black leather skirt the size of an eye-patch. A six-inch cigarette holder was pursed in her lips.

I whispered to Sarah, 'She's lowering the tone a bit, isn't she?'

'What about those two couples?' said Sarah softly, jerking her head in the direction of a table to our left.

They definitely looked odd. One woman

had on a shimmering pink satin cocktail dress, her partner was wearing a brown tweed jacket. They seemed to be trying to give the impression that they were husband and wife, yet they could *not* have got dressed together to go out for the evening. The other woman was wearing a white satin blouse and a black skirt that barely reached the knee.

We had not liberated our knees to the mini yet. A glimpse of knee at this time would cause embarrassment, and the knee would be swiftly covered. No such embarrassment at the Peacock tonight.

Her partner had on a navy blue blazer and grey flannels. He took a card from his inside pocket and passed it to satin blouse. She read it, smiled, said something and passed it to her girl friend to read. I heard her say something about him having a well-paid job.

Throughout the evening I was intrigued at the different manoeuvres of the women that took place at the next table. I gave a furtive glance at pink satin – she was stealthily raising the skirt of her dress inch by inch. Meanwhile, white satin had undone yet another button of her blouse.

Tweed jacket had developed a facial twitch and kept twirling the gold band on his left hand nervously. Blue blazer was confident, assertive; his voice became louder and louder as he pontificated about his sales record and regular trips to San Francisco.

The two couples stood up simultaneously, as if they had received a signal, linked arms and left.

As Roy and I walked towards the bar, he to pay the bill, I to go to the toilet, he was propositioned by the blonde at the bar, despite the fact that it was obvious that we were together.

'Are you with anyone tonight, darling?' she purred. Roy ignored her.

As I let go his arm to go to the ladies room, a man at the bar brushed against me. 'Doing anything tonight, love?'

I couldn't get out of the Peacock quickly enough and, grabbing Sarah, we disappeared outside to wait for Vernon and Roy.

'I'm glad we took Miss Harris there for lunch and not for an evening meal,' said Sarah.

'Me too.'

Through the glass door we watched as Vernon and Roy chatted quietly to each other and grinned, as though they were planning something.

'Sarah,' said Vernon with a straight face, 'what sort of a girl *are* you, to go to this low-down place?'

'Monika,' began Roy, 'fancy you taking us to this pick-up joint. What *type* of girls are you?'

We were stunned into silence as they continued.

'Do you know, Roy, these girls go out every night in black stockings and nurses' uniforms. We *think* they are going out to some poor dying patient, when all the time they are going to the Peacock to strut their stuff.'

Vernon couldn't keep a straight face much longer and burst out laughing. We all linked arms together and, laughing, made our way to the underground.

Chapter Twenty-seven

'How can I just let you go, man, just like that? You just walking out my life, Sal? Study, study, study is all I hear from you. All this driving me mad.'

'Vern, calm down. I've only been trying to get you to take things seriously. It's no good shouting like this.'

'What all the hurry for, girl?'

Sarah went quiet, then she spoke gently. 'I've got my papers through today. In six to ten weeks I will be sailing to Canada.'

'Sal, you can't leave me like this, go off on your own.'

'Vern, what have I been saying all this time? You knew I was going, with or without you.'

'I didn't think you really meant it,' said Vernon, looking dejected.

'I'm not playing games, man. You know me well. When my mind is made up, I do it.'

Vernon walked over to the door. 'My mind is made up too. Find someone else to give your orders to.'

Without looking back, he left, slamming the door behind him.

'Do you think he means it?' I asked.

'He'll be back,' Sarah said calmly. 'Look Mik, if he loves me, he'll follow me.'

'What date did you say?'

'Not sure yet, the letter says six to ten weeks, then I will be given a sailing date.'

'What part of Canada?'

'Saskatchewan. I didn't get my preference. Maybe I'll get to move to Calgary later. Promise me something, Mik: watch over Vern for me. You will need to make him get down to studying.'

'I'll make him settle down to it,' I said.

A month later, there had been no sign or word from Vernon. Sarah was beginning to get anxious.

'What you think, Mik? Do you think he's really gone for good?'

'No, where would he go? You know Vernon, the optimum drama in a situation like this. He will probably burst in just as you are leaving to get the ship.'

'Oh I hope not, I hope he comes back before too late.'

'He's hoping you will change your mind

and not go,' I said.

'If that's his game, he's out of luck.'

One of my visits that day was to a 'sticky fingered' household. As soon as I knocked on the door, the household was thrown into a frenzied activity of slamming cupboard doors and the sound of drawers shoved quickly on their runners. A pair of eyes peered through the letter box. There was a permanent crease in the curtain at the front window where it had been used as a lookout post. A hand pulled back the beige cotton curtain and tried to surreptitiously look to see who was at the door.

'Will yer shut it when I tell yer,' came a woman's voice.

The light was on upstairs, and another boy's face appeared at the net curtain.

'Will you all shut up. It's only the bloody nurse,' said a boy whose voice had broken.

'Shut up the lot of yer. Someone let her in.'

A young girl about ten years opened the door.

'Mum says you can come in.'

There's nothing quite like the friendly welcome that one gets at the Bentleys', I thought as I stepped inside. The panic wouldn't be over yet, children were still stuffing objects under cushions, others feigned innocence and made out to be reading the *Beano* or the *Dandy*.

'It's OK, luv. It's yer blue coat, we fought you was the Old Bill. When the old man's inside like, yer gets a bit nervous when yer sees someone looking like a copper at the door.'

Mrs Bentley moved a pile of ironing off the armchair.

'Sit down, nurse. 'ave a cuppa. 'enery, get the nurse a bit o' me cake.'

Before I had a chance to protest, a large piece of iced cake landed on a plate in my lap.

'It's me birthday, see. I'm thirty-four. Not bad, eh? Nine kids and one grankid.'

'Congratulations,' I said. 'It's my birthday today too.'

'Well I never, you a Gemini like meself. I always reads me stars. Us Geminis are s'posed to be two different people rolled into one. Rosie, go get Mum's stuff for her jab, nurse is busy.'

'Mum, is Uncle Pete coming today?' asked the boy with the *Beano*.

'Ssh, read yer comic, it's none of yer business,' said Mrs Bentley.

'Uncle Pete, giz us money to go to the flicks,' he continued.

'I told yer, keep quiet, yer little sod. Sorry, nurse, 'scuse my French, but he can be a right little bleeder sometimes, asking questions.'

'Ouch! Shit, that cat's clawed my leg,' said

the boy from behind the *Dandy*.

'Stop that swearing at once, in front of company. I don't know where yer gets all yer bloody swearing from. It can't be from 'ome.'

Children that were born immediately after 1945 were lightheartedly referred to as 'war relief'. Every time that Mr Bentley was released from 'Her Majesty's School for Heavy Needlework', another Bentley baby was spawned. The Bentley kids were what could be called 'prison relief'. This time, judging by Mrs Bentley's increased girth, there already looked to be a not so happy event in about three months.

As I rose to leave, Mrs Bentley took my arm.

'Come 'ere, nurse. I believe in being good to those what's been good to me. 'ere, 'elp yerself to a little something for yer birthday.'

Mrs Bentley pulled opened the door of one of the tall recess cupboards that was fixed either side of the fireplace. It was an Aladdin's cave of toiletries and perfumes. Attractive boxes all colours and sizes were stacked high. Yardley, Coty, Revlon and Max Factor were just a few. I took the smallest insignificant-looking box I could find, a box of four Morny, bath cubes.

'Bath cubes is no good, go get a bag for nurse.'

'No really, this will do fine, thank you very much,' I said. I edged towards the front door, but Mrs Bentley blocked my exit in the hallway.

'Can I talk to you personal like?'

'Of course.'

'You know my old man's inside for armed robbery? 'e's coming 'ome next Friday.'

'Yes, I heard he was coming out.'

'My old man says 'is best mate Pete stitched 'im up when 'e got sent down. Yer know what it's like, yer gets lonely wivout a bloke around. Pete's been good to me and the kids. I don't know 'ow to say it but ... I'm 'aving Pete's baby.'

'These things happen–' I started.

Some people that already live chaotic lives, delight in spicing things up a bit, determined to dice with danger and make a drama out of a crisis.

'My Dickie's got a foul temper when 'e gets going. I thought if you're not doing anyfink on Friday you could come round, for what they call moral somefink?'

'Moral support?'

'Yeah, that's it.'

Immoral support more like it, I thought. She must be joking.

'No, I'm sorry Mrs Bentley, I won't be here next week. I'm away in Scotland,' I lied.

On my return home, Sarah was waving a letter from Roy. I took it into the bedroom to read. The atmosphere had been a bit tense with Vernon off the scene. One of Sarah's West Indian friends had spoken to me in Brixton. She reckoned that she had seen Vernon with a black girl from his office, called Lara. I knew it would upset Sarah if it reached her ears; besides it could mean nothing and just have been an innocent meeting. I wasn't sure whether she had heard any rumours. Regardless, she had thrown herself into her preparations for Canada. The sewing machine had been in constant use making outfit after outfit. She hadn't mentioned Vernon's name all week.

I sat on my bed and opened the envelope. Roy's opening word of endearment gave an immediate jolt.

My dearest Monika,

As you know, I have been away on a helicopter course. We got into difficulties and narrowly missed some rocky terrain and caused damage to the helicopter. At the time I thought my number was on it. I thought about you Monika, and realised I might never see you again. I decided then and there that if I got out of it alive, I was going to ask you to marry me. It is something that I had been thinking about for some time.

Strange, it took an accident for me to find you and another to nearly lose you. As you know, I finish my time in the RAF March next year. How about a spring wedding?

Monika please don't keep me waiting too long for an answer. If you decide that I am not the one for you I will be heartbroken. (I will probably chuck myself off Putney Bridge ... I'm only joking.)

Roy finished it with a poem that he said he had written himself:

When first we met I gave my heart
I hoped and prayed we'd never part.
And by your eyes so bonny green
I swear I'm yours forever.
And with my lips I seal this vow
And break it shall I never.

My hands shook as I read the letter. I held it close to me and sighed. Everything would change now. Nothing would ever be the same.

'Are you all right in there? You're very quiet.'

'I'm fine, I've got some good news,' I said, as I opened the door. 'Roy has asked me to marry him next year.'

'Kid, that's wonderful. And about time too. What took him so long anyway? You must let me make your trousseau. We must have a party. A double celebration.'

'A double?'

Sarah's face lit up and she grinned as she

waved her left hand under my nose.

'I thought you'd never notice. I've been permanently left-handed all afternoon. Vern came round in his lunch break and brought me this.' A solitaire diamond ring sparkled on her third finger.

We hugged and congratulated each other. I was so glad that Vernon had returned. Despite her cheerful disposition, I knew that the past few weeks had been very anxious ones for her.

'In fact as soon as your Roy can get off, we can have a triple party. Two engagements and a farewell party.'

With all the excitement, the last remark dropped like a stone slab. Instantly, I was back in the nurses' Preliminary Training School and could hear the Sister Tutor's warning in her introduction to nursing: *After you qualify, several will stay, but many will leave. Some of you will return to your own countries, others will go abroad and carve out new careers. In this profession you will make many friends from all over the world. But you will <u>lose</u> as many friends as you make.*

These words had never been so poignant as they were now.

Sarah and I had confided in each other about our love lives. We had laughed until we had cried. We had comforted each other when we were upset. We had shared our lives, yet we would not be at each other's weddings. We would soon go our separate ways and we might never see each other again.

Chapter Twenty-eight

'For God sake, how many more labels do you need? I must have written twenty already.'

'Eh, what, what did you say?' Sarah called from the kitchen.

I shouted back, 'LABELS, how many more LABELS?'

'Everything has to be marked, do a few more just in case.'

'I know one thing, if I didn't know how to spell Saskatoon, Saskatchewan before, I certainly know now.'

Sarah's head appeared around the kitchen door and in an affected voice said, 'I have finished your trousseau AGAIN. I really don't know what all the fuss was about. One would expect one to wear something a bit see-through on one's wedding night, wouldn't one?'

'Thanks very much Sarah, the nylon negligees are really lovely. But they are so sheer, they must be about five denier. The frilly lace at the top and bottom has made a difference, but there is still rather a lot of naked flesh in between.'

'Listen girl, I think you a bit of a prude. Is this for your honeymoon night? Or are you marching down Oxford Street in it? What you worry about *five* denier? Roy will be like a walking hormone. If he anything of a man, it will be off in *five* seconds.' She handed me a pink paper parcel.

'Don't worry about tidying up, Sarah, I can do that when you have gone.'

'You *are* coming to see me off, aren't you?'

'With Vernon going, I thought you might like to be on your own.'

'What do *you think*, girl? When Vern sort himself out, I shall have a lifetime with him. Of course you must come. Knowing Vernon, he will need a shoulder to cry on.'

Sarah had a midwifery sister's job waiting for her in Canada. Vernon was still struggling to get down to studying, having flunked one of his exams in accountancy already.

We set off for the embarkation dock at Tilbury and made our way to the quayside.

'If you love me, Vern, you won't fool away your time, man, you'll get those books out every night. Otherwise, you no good to me.'

'Don't be so hard, Sal,' said Vernon plaintively.

'It's no good moaning. I don't intend to support you.'

I gave her a hug and kissed her goodbye, fighting to hold back the tears. What was that she'd called me ... *a blue-eyed soul sister*.

We would both take our different paths. We would promise to write. We would hope to see each other again. In my heart I knew that would probably never happen. We had shared a unique friendship, that neither time nor distance would allow us to forget.

Vernon and Sarah hugged and kissed each other passionately, Vernon clinging to her until the very last moment and Sarah having to pull herself free.

As the ship slipped away, the crowd surged forward. The passengers leaned over the rail, waved and shouted. Others blew kisses and waved handkerchiefs. Those who weren't waving them had buried their eyes in them. We were surrounded by soft sobbing and sniffing. We waved. We smiled our fake smiles. Gradually the ship looked like a sea-gull sleeping on the horizon and bobbing gently until it was a white feather. It was gone, leaving us feeling bereft.

Sarah was right about Vernon needing a shoulder to cry on. He would come over to the flat and loll about like a love-sick loon. Every day it was the same old cry: 'I'm never going to make it, Mik.'

'Of course you are. Pull yourself together, you can't go on like this. How do you expect to concentrate on your studies when you don't eat anything?'

One Sunday I cooked him a West Indian dish of curried goat and rice. He pushed it away after a few mouthfuls. His athletic body was pared away like an onion skin to reveal a small lifeless shell. Even Miss Harris started baking and feeding him shortbread and leaving him a huge bagful to take home.

'I've put extra butter in it, to try and fatten him up,' she said to me.

If he arrived too early and the library was still open for an hour or two, I would send him off with his books to study.

It all paid off one day when an ecstatic Vernon punched the air and dangled a brown envelope marked Goldsmiths College, University of London. He didn't exactly shout *veni, vidi, vici*, it was, 'I've made it, I've got it, I've passed.'

That was good enough for me. 'Thank God for that,' I said with genuine relief.

Miss Harris invited us into her flat and she had opened a bottle of Asti Spumante. We congratulated and toasted him and wished him well.

Needless to say, within a few weeks I was writing out more Saskatoon, Saskatchewan labels. Sarah, while waiting for Vernon had been trying to put out feelers for jobs.

They were re-united. He eventually got a job, but it was four hundred miles away.

This meant that they could only see each other at weekends.

'This old place won't be the same,' said Miss Harris, 'without you and Sarah. I shall miss you all. First Sarah then Vernon and now you are off. Pity Sarah had to leave before the wedding. But I'll be there. We must keep in touch. If it hadn't been for my friend, I wonder if Sarah...?' Miss Harris looked deep in thought.

'Did you ever think about getting married, Miss Harris?'

'I *was* married once. I was only eighteen. It was war-time – Tom was a pilot. In fact your fiancé reminded me of him. He had managed to get a twenty-four-hour pass. On the spur of the moment he got a special licence and we were married the same day. We were so excited. We spent our honeymoon, just one night and one day, at Brighton. We couldn't go on the beach, there were warning signs: *KEEP OFF – LAND MINES.* There was barbed wire everywhere. We didn't care, we were just happy to be together.' As she spoke she fingered a tiny gold ring on the little finger of her left hand.

'It was six months before I saw him again,' she said. 'He had left behind a slim young bride, and now I was expecting a baby. I looked so fat, so ugly but Tom was wonderful. *You look marvellous*, he said. *Just be proud that you are carrying our baby.*

'I had got a couple of rooms in a house nearby, with a lovely couple. Tom visited when he could. Three weeks later I was waiting for Tom to return to base. He had been out on a mission and his plane had been shot up. As he came in to land it was obvious his engine was on fire. Tom was burnt to death. I went into acute shock.' Miss Harris dabbed her eyes with her handkerchief as she spoke.

'I'm so sorry, I had no idea.'

'Then when I lost the baby, I just wanted to end it all. I was inconsolable. I wept for days. One day I woke up and I asked myself who was I crying for. For Tom, the baby, or myself? ... I was weeping for myself.'

I put my arm around her and softly said, 'I'm sorry, Miss Harris, I shouldn't have asked you that question.'

She gave a big sigh. 'It's all in a lifetime, Monika. My life is like a pocket watch. I don't keep on taking it out and telling everyone the time. But if anyone asks me, I will take it out and tell them.'

She abruptly changed the subject.

'Are you going home tomorrow?'

'Not tomorrow, I have to say goodbye to Miss Wright.'

'I thought you girls didn't like the Superintendent.'

'I think we all were a bit in awe of her at first, but I've learned a lot from her: tolerance, patience and the need for people to feel needed. We were her family and now, as a member of the family, I am flying the nest. I need to say goodbye.'

There was a lump in my throat as I said my farewells to my colleagues and to Miss Wright. I put my Gladstone bag back on the shelf and wheeled my bike into the shed.

I had qualified as a Queen's Nursing Sister and I was about to spread my wings. Tonight would be my last night in London. I had a post of District Nursing Sister in my hometown in Kent. The Ambulance Service had promised to teach me how to drive. Later I would be issued with my own car, an Austin Mini.

Suitcases and boxes were lined up ready in the hall. I looked around the flat that had been my home for two years, with more than a tinge of sadness.

There on top of the wardrobe, I had almost forgotten, was Sarah's pink parcel. I decided to try on the pink see-through creation. I couldn't help smiling. In addition to the frilly lace, it had now acquired three minute black roses. Sewn on at three strategic points!

The publishers hope that this book has given you enjoyable reading. Large Print Books are especially designed to be as easy to see and hold as possible. If you wish a complete list of our books please ask at your local library or write directly to:

Magna Large Print Books
Magna House, Long Preston,
Skipton, North Yorkshire.
BD23 4ND

This Large Print Book, for people
who cannot read normal print,
is published under the auspices of

THE ULVERSCROFT FOUNDATION

... we hope you have enjoyed this book.
Please think for a moment about those
who have worse eyesight than you ...
and are unable to even read or enjoy
Large Print without great difficulty.

You can help them by sending a
donation, large or small, to:

**The Ulverscroft Foundation,
1, The Green, Bradgate Road,
Anstey, Leicestershire, LE7 7FU,
England.**
or request a copy of our brochure for
more details.

The Foundation will use all donations
to assist those people who are visually
impaired and need special attention
with medical research, diagnosis
and treatment.

Thank you very much for your help.

Mrs Southgate

p-m a m